"The sun looks down on nothing half so good as a household laughing together over a meal."
-C.S. Lewis, *The Weight of Glory*

The CHURCH POTLUCK

by Nathan Aufenkamp

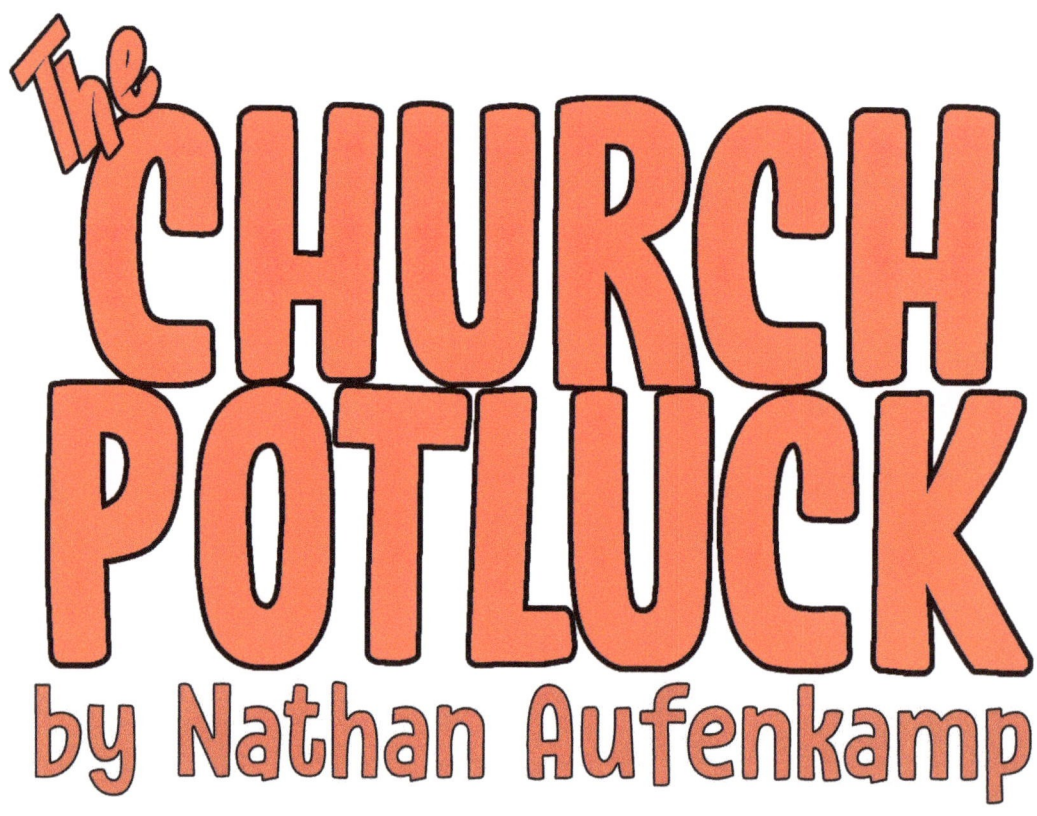

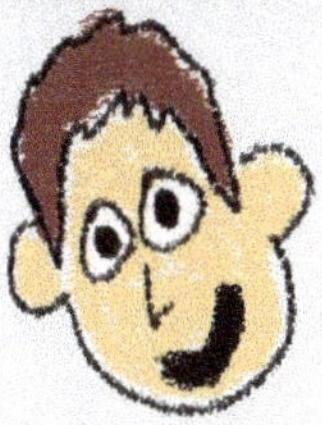

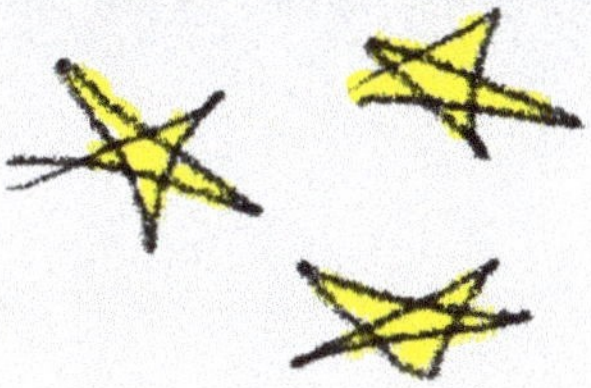

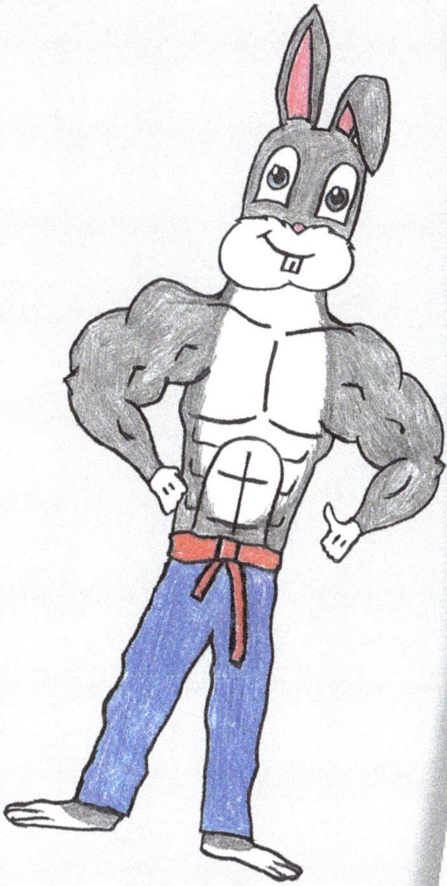

As long as I can remember, I've been doodling on every piece of scrap paper I could find. If you went through my homework from any age, you'd find my drawings in the margins of just about every page. I probably drew more cartoons in social studies and math than I did in art class. Another thing I love is making people laugh. Doing anything and everything to get a chuckle. And if it's during a point when we shouldn't be laughing, well that makes it all the more funny. Tie all that together with my love for God, love for the Bible, and the fact that I'm a pastor's kid, and you get The Church Potluck. A collection of cartoons and comics mostly consisting of Bible and church humor. You'll laugh, you'll smirk, and some you'll just shake your head and groan at. And who knows, there might be a couple you'll have to crack open your Bible for. Whatever the case is, grab your pan of scotcharoos and enjoy The Church Potluck.

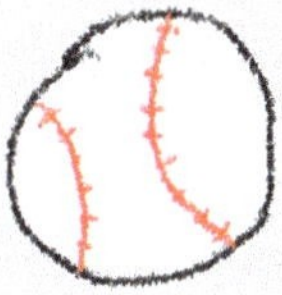

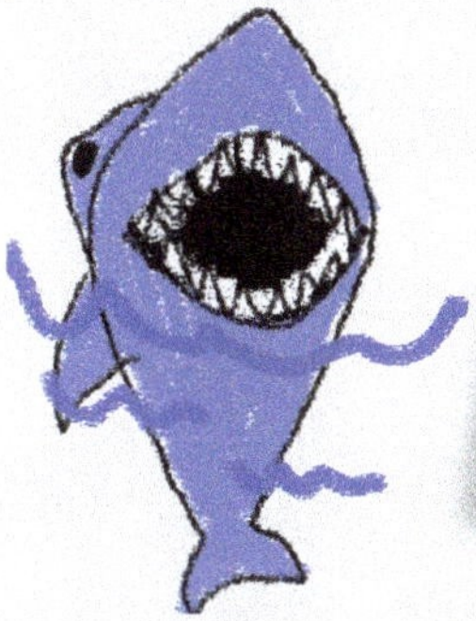

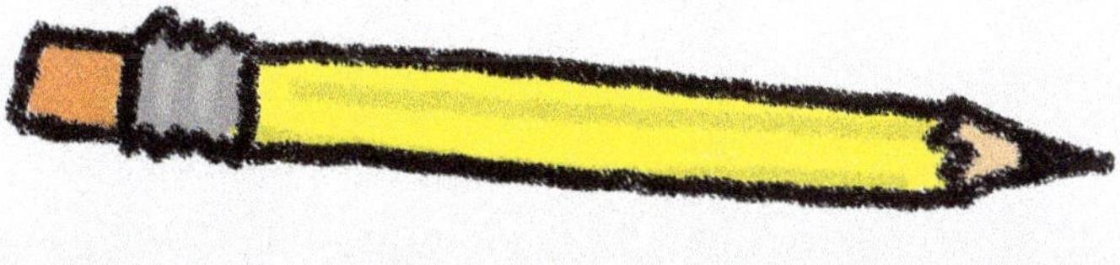

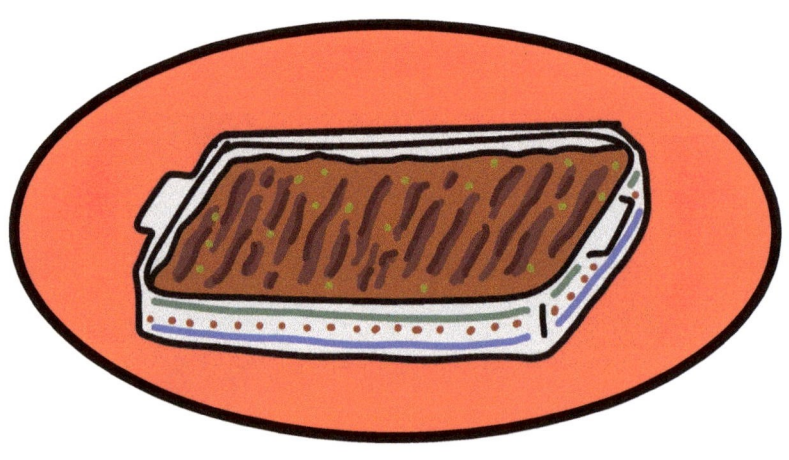

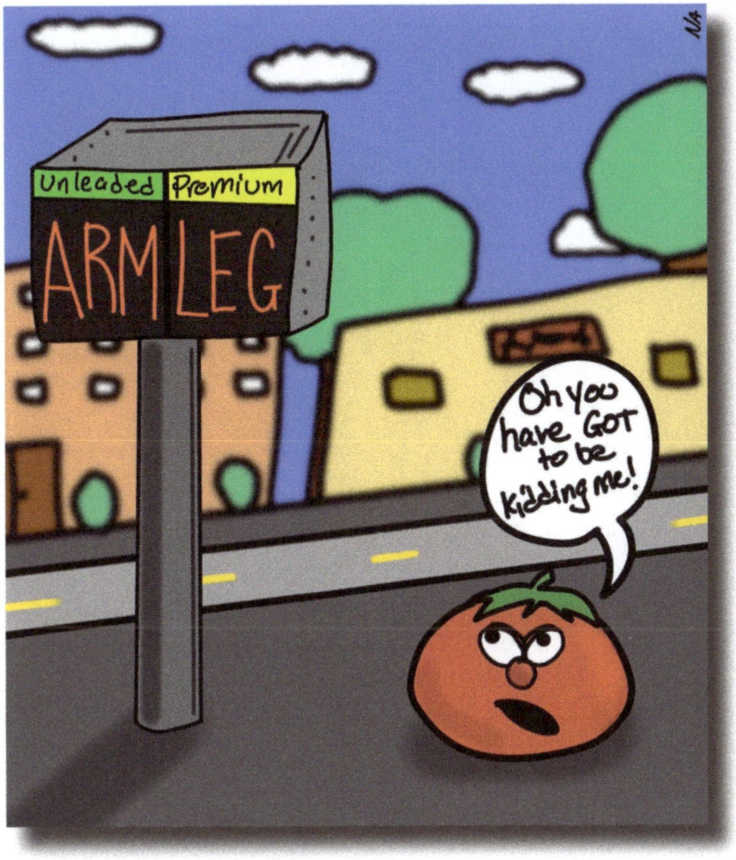
Unleaded
Premium
ARM
LEG
Oh you have GOT to be kidding me!

Bob the Tomato is sick of rising gas prices.

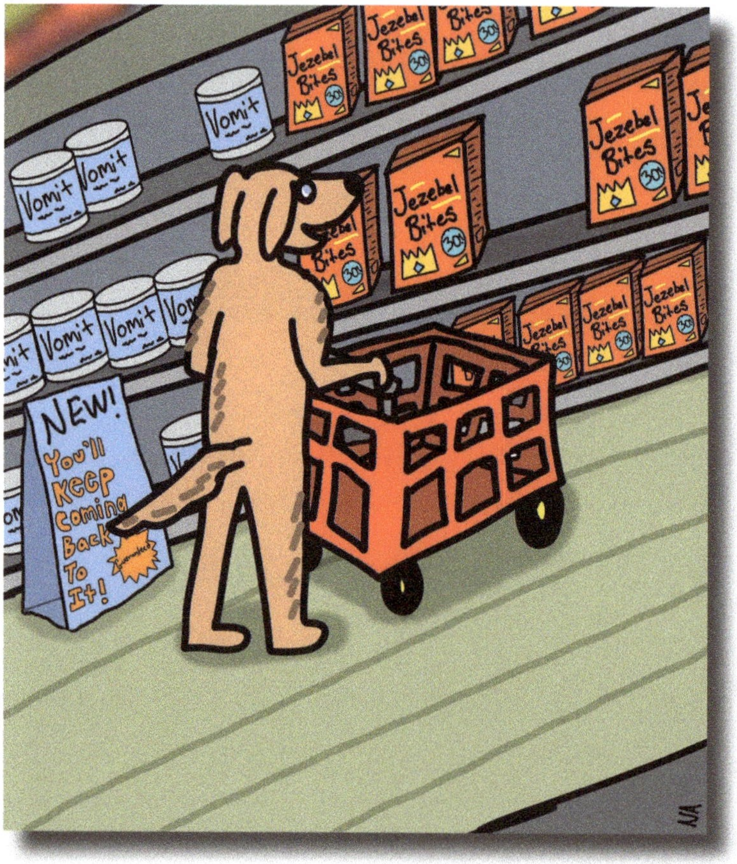
Jezebel Bites
Vomit
NEW!
You'll Keep Coming Back To It!

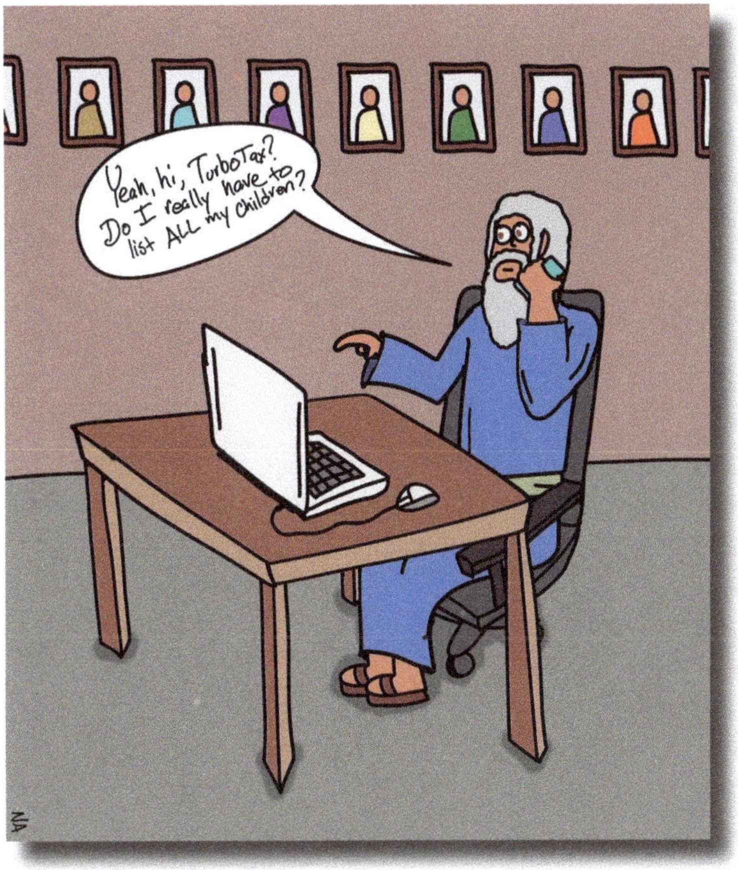
Yeah, hi, TurboTax? Do I really have to list ALL my children?

Abraham does his taxes.

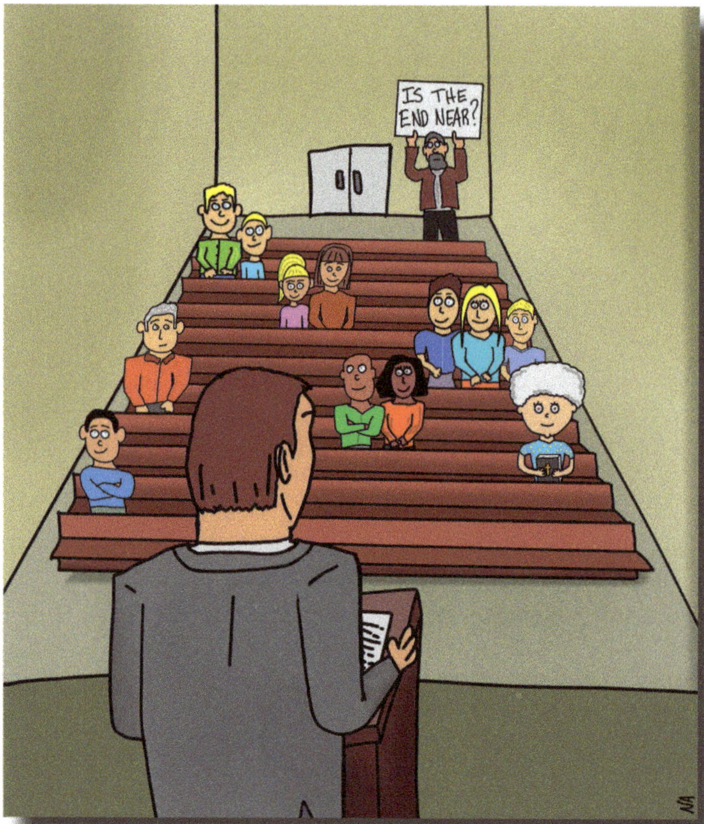
IS THE
END NEAR?

Pastor Bill didn't realize how long his sermons were getting until the man from the corner down the street started coming to church.

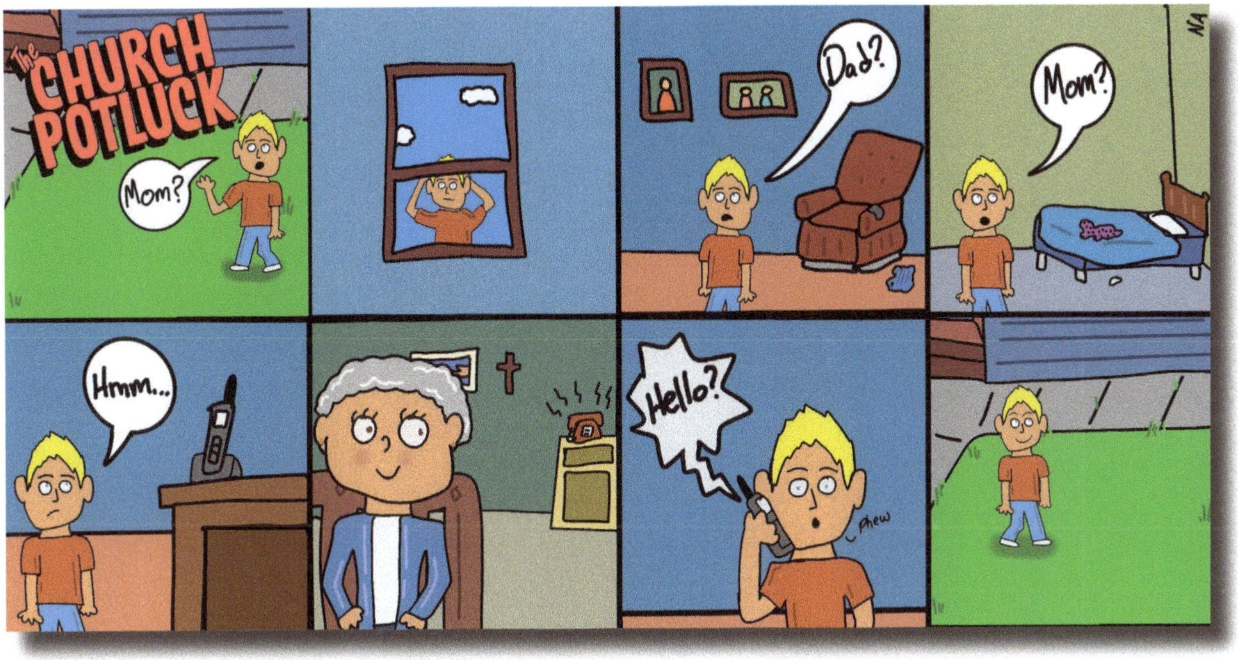
The CHURCH POTLUCK
Mom?
Dad?
Mom?
NA
Hmm...
Hello?
Phew

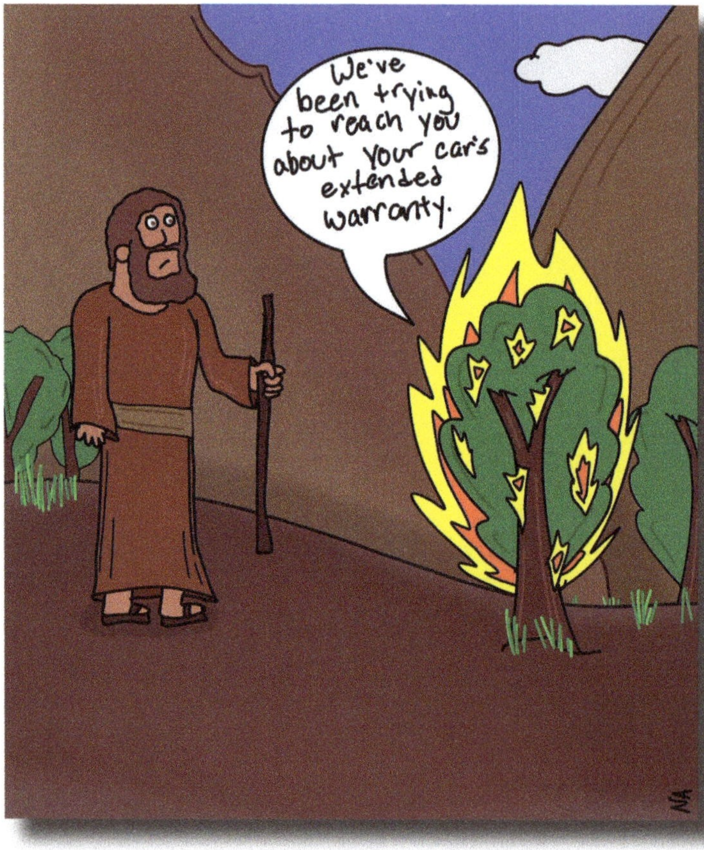
We've been trying to reach you about your car's extended warranty.

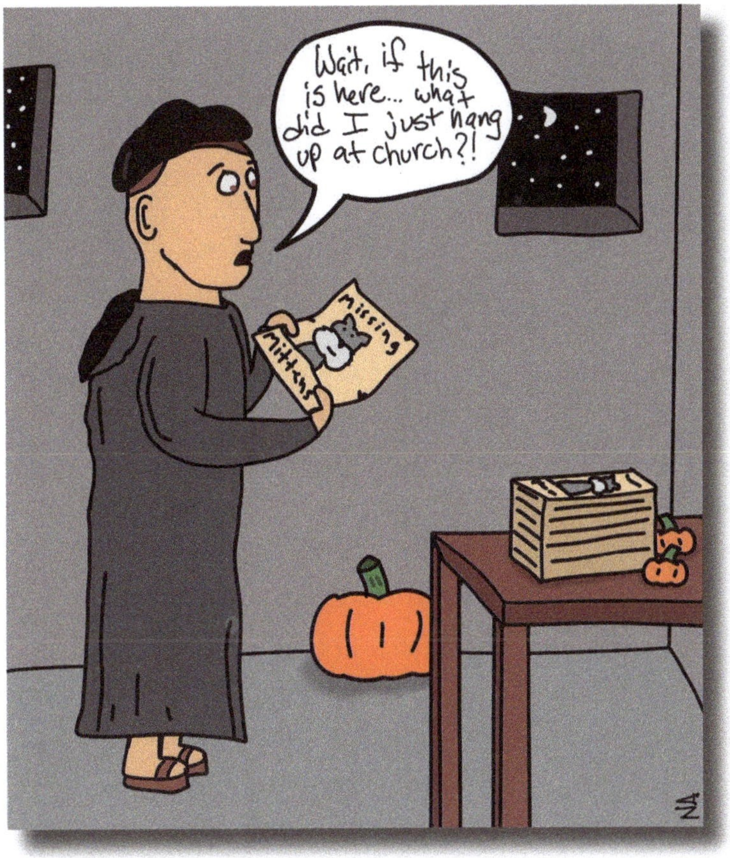
Wait, if this is here... what did I just hang up at church?!
Missing
Mittens

Martin Luther arrives home and makes a startling realization.

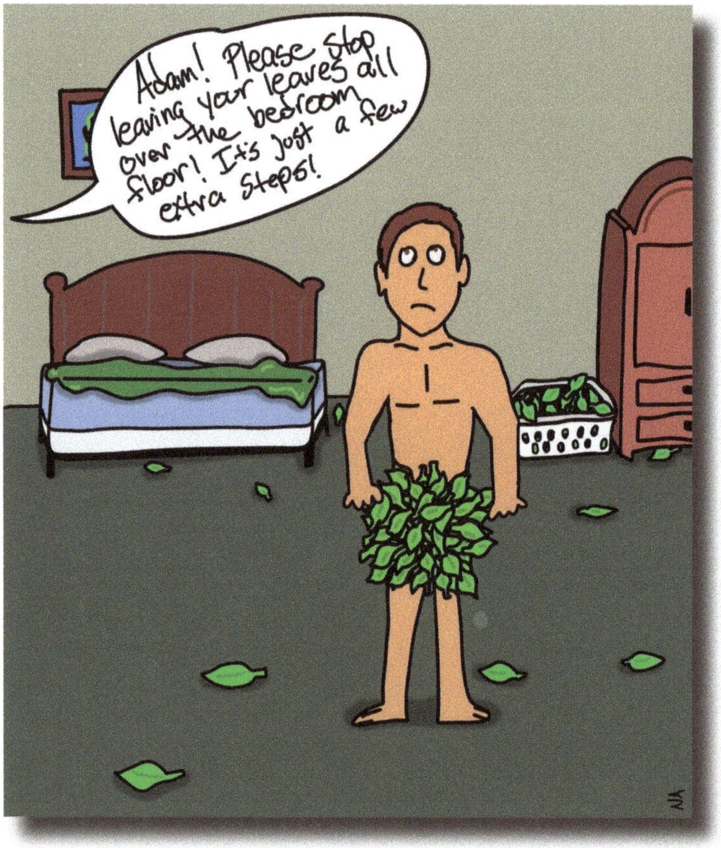
Adam! Please stop leaving your leaves all over the bedroom floor! It's just a few extra steps!

Trouble in paradise.

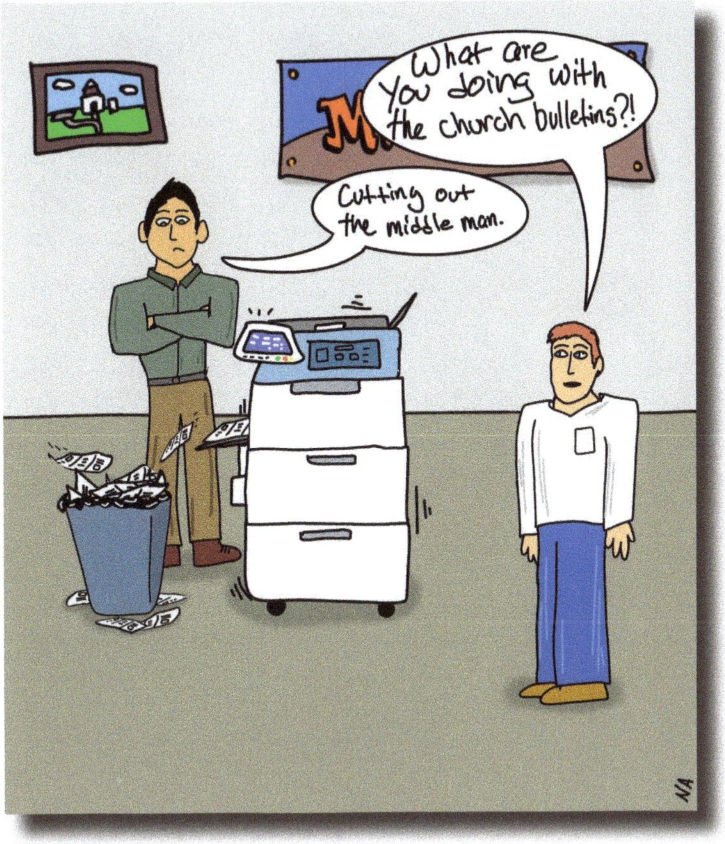
What are you doing with the church bulletins?!
Cutting out the middle man.
NA

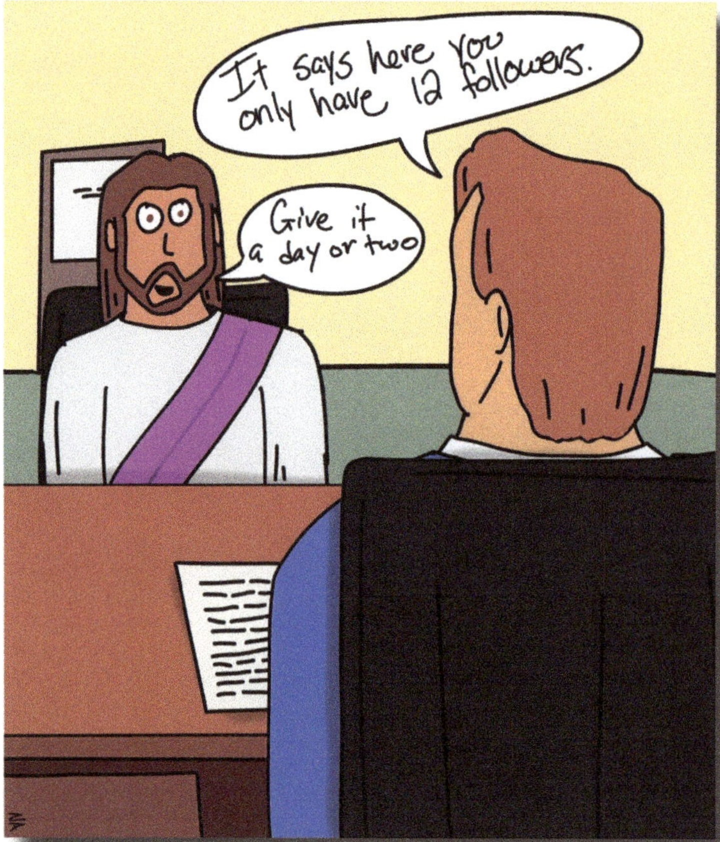
It says here you only have 12 followers.
Give it a day or two

Jesus applies to be a social media manager.

Ezekiel sits down to a hearty meal.

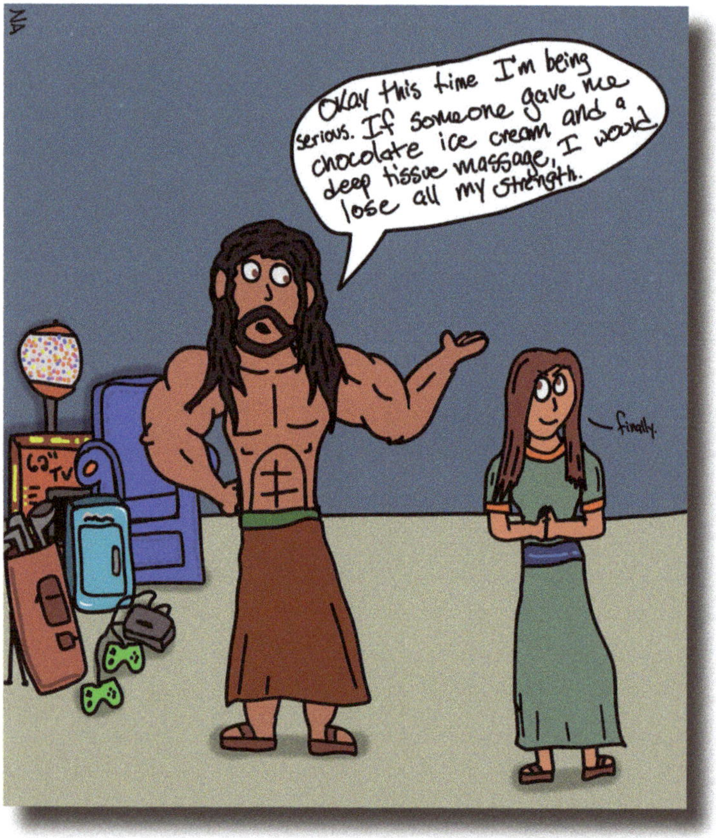
NA
Okay this time I'm being serious. If someone gave me chocolate ice cream and a deep tissue massage, I would lose all my strength.
62" TV
finally.

Once Samson realized what Delilah was up to he decided to make the most of it.

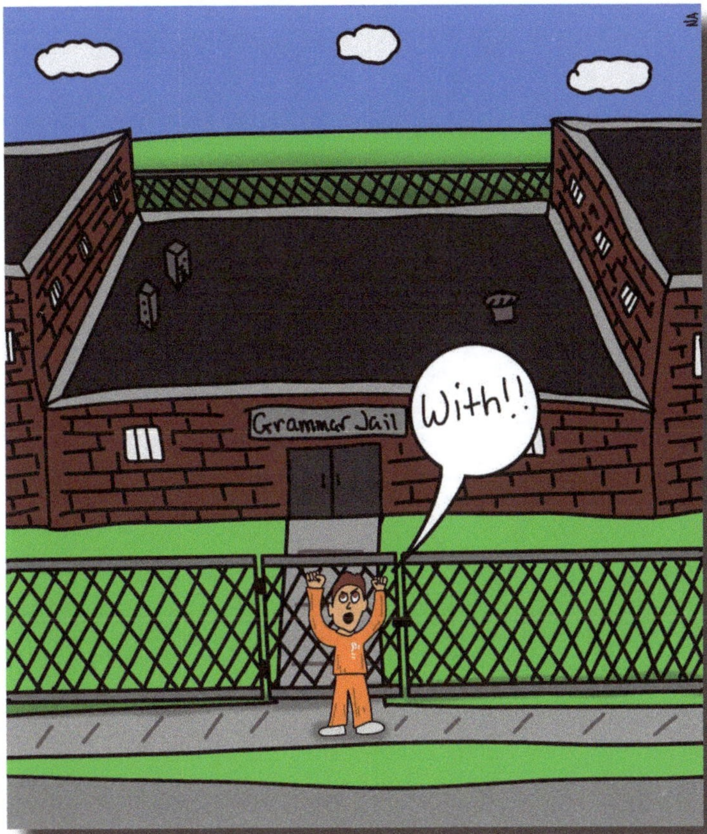
Grammar Jail
With!!

After years of being locked up by the grammar police, Mike proves them all wrong by once and for all ending a sentence with a preposition.

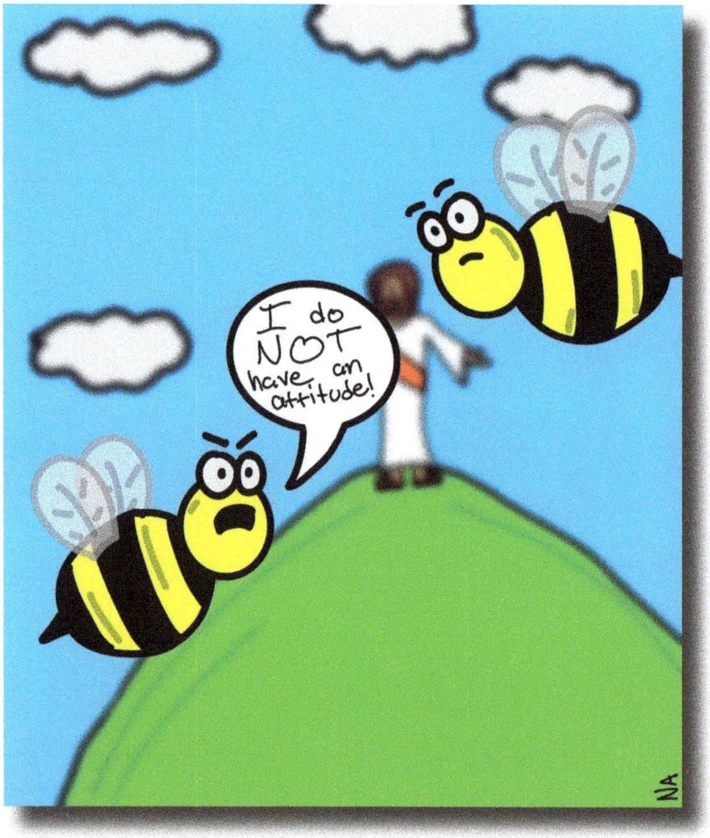
I do NOT have an attitude!
NA

A couple of bees sit in on the
Sermon on the Mount.

Jack and Jill went up the hill, one disappeared, one left standing still.

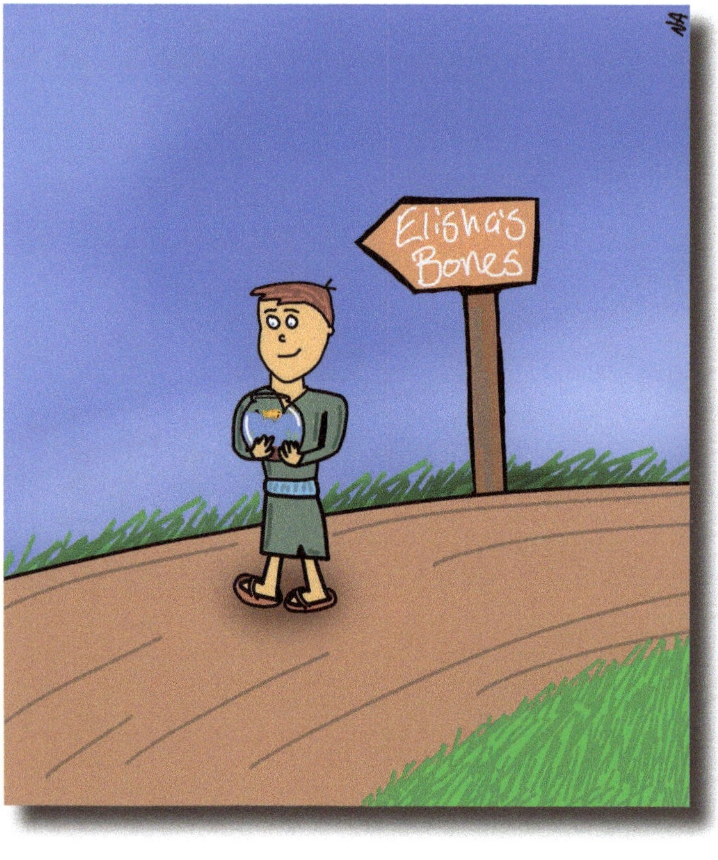
Elisha's
Bones

Delivering the punchline.

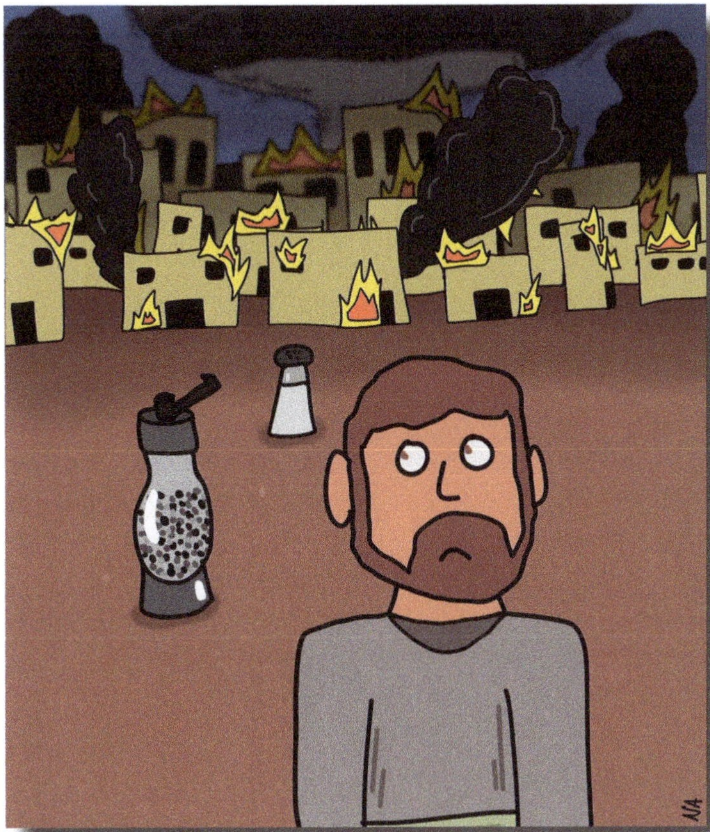
NA

Bible scholars recently uncovered proof of Lot's estranged cousin, Jerry, who also looked back and instead turned into a giant pepper grinder.

Valentine's Day was easily Solomon's least favorite holiday.

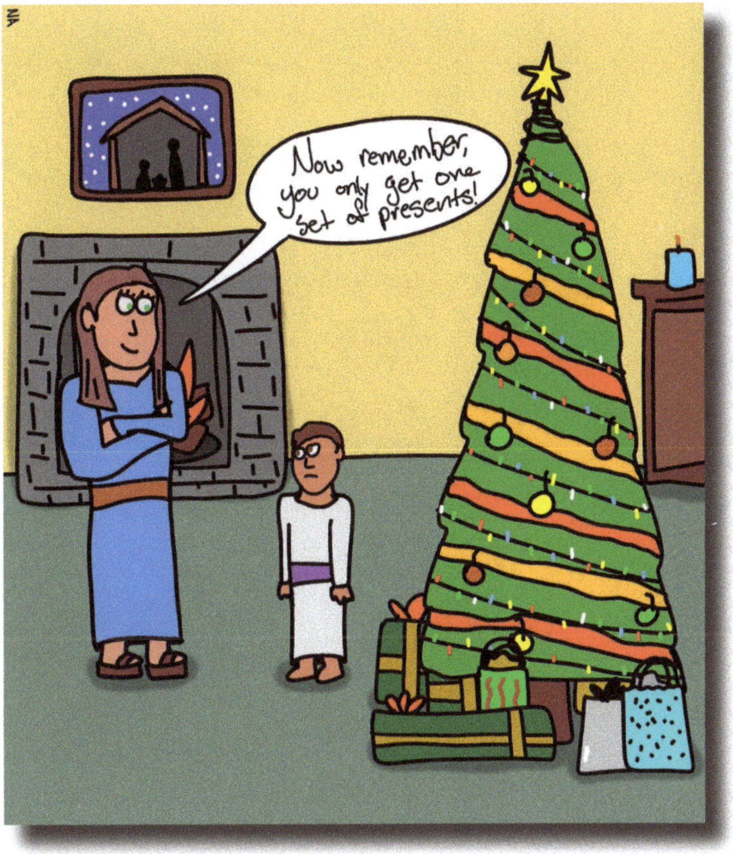
Now remember, you only get one set of presents!

Mary sets some ground rules.

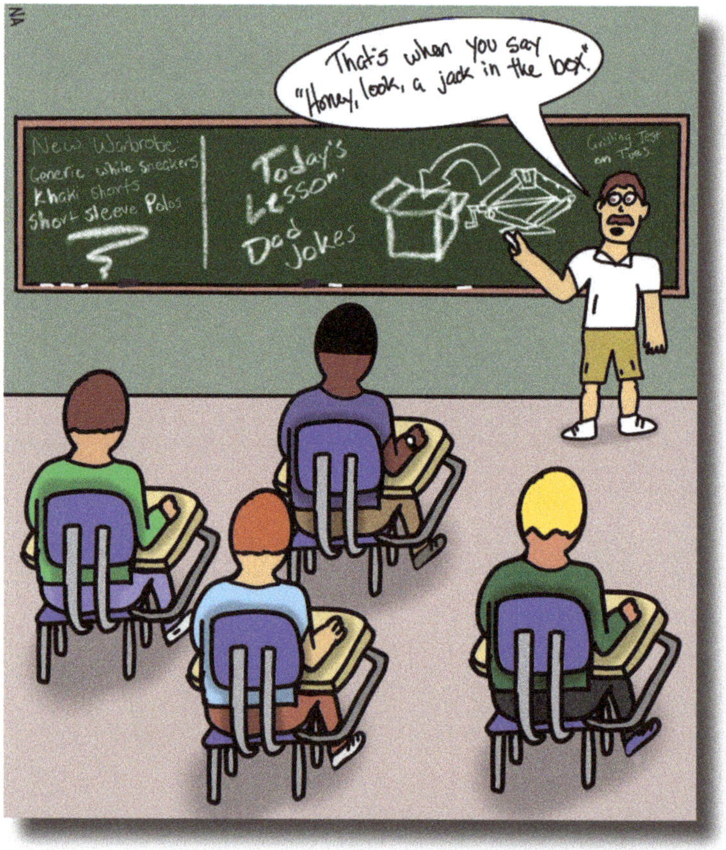
NA
That's when you say "Honey, look, a jack in the box".
New Warbrobe
Generic white sneakers
Khaki Shorts
Short sleeve Polos
Today's Lesson:
Dad Jokes
Grilling Test on Tues

New Dad University.

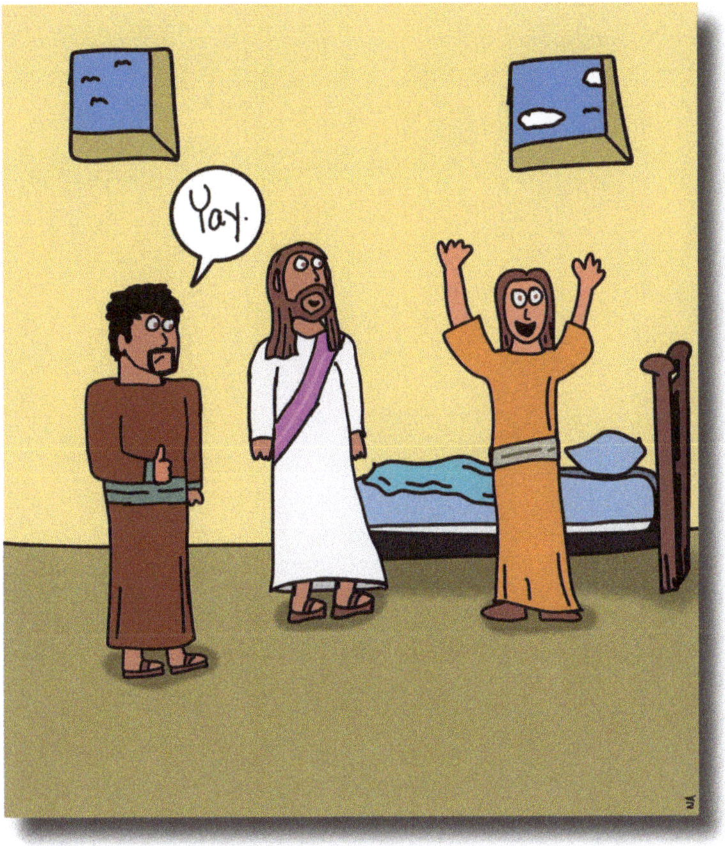
Yay.

Peter could hardly contain his excitement
when Jesus healed his mother-in-law.

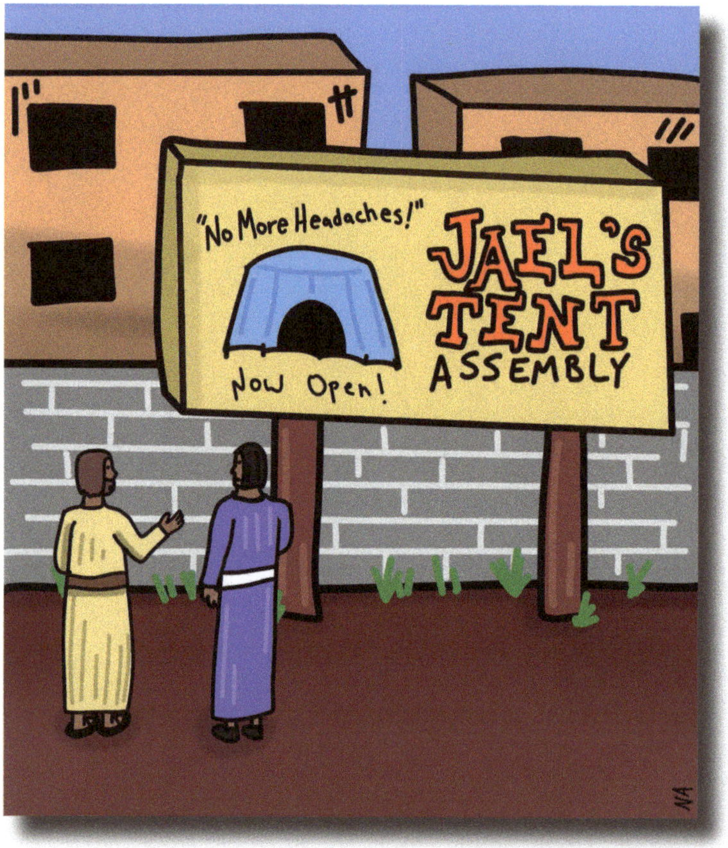
"No More Headaches!"
Now Open!
JAEL'S TENT ASSEMBLY

"I feel as though this is in poor taste."

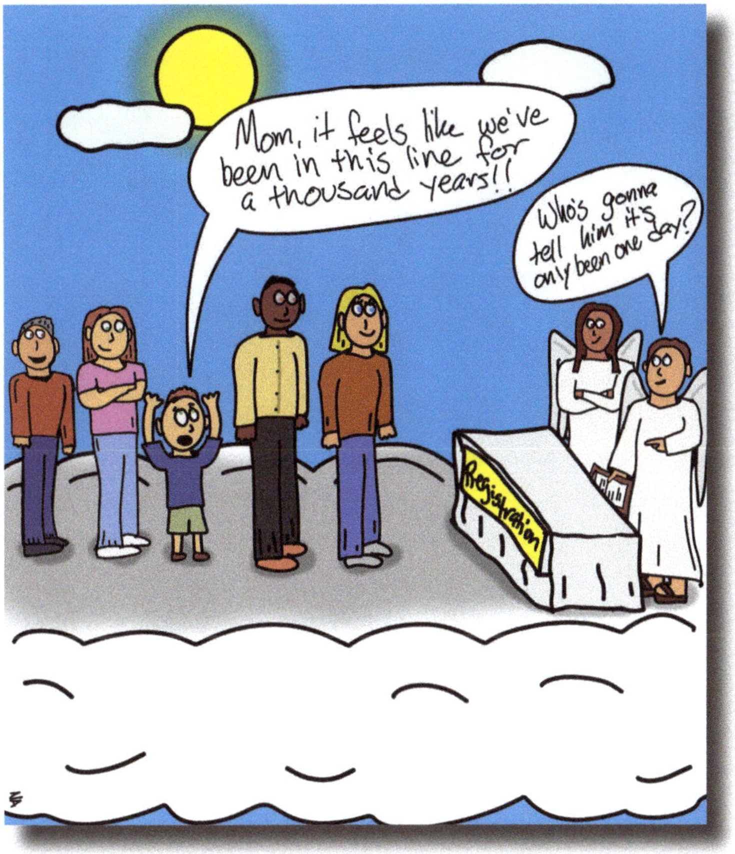
Mom, it feels like we've been in this line for a thousand years!!
Who's gonna tell him it's only been one day?
Registration

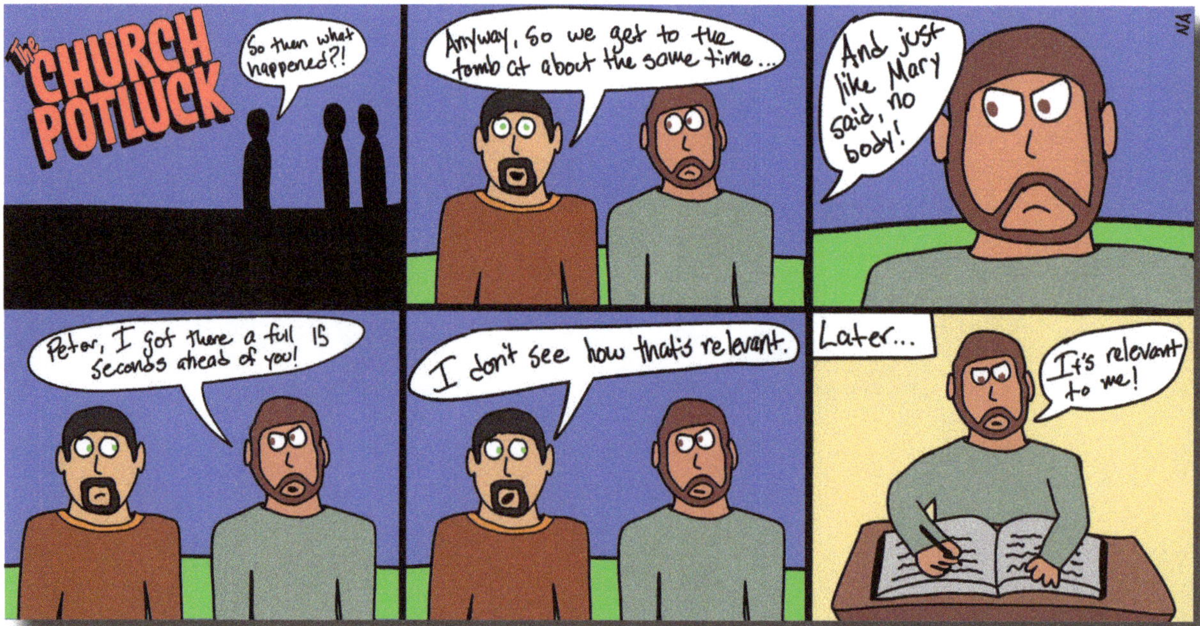
The CHURCH POTLUCK
So then what happened?!
Anyway, so we get to the tomb at about the same time...
And just like Mary said, no body!
NA
Peter, I got there a full 15 seconds ahead of you!
I don't see how that's relevant.
Later...
It's relevant to me!

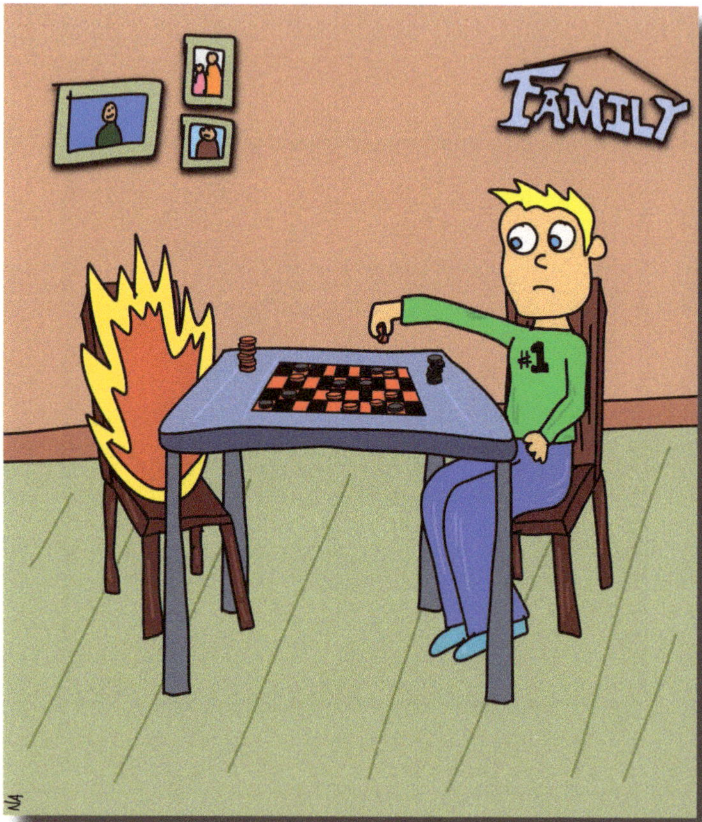
FAMILY
#1

Bobby's mother warned him several times but
he always had so much fun playing with fire.

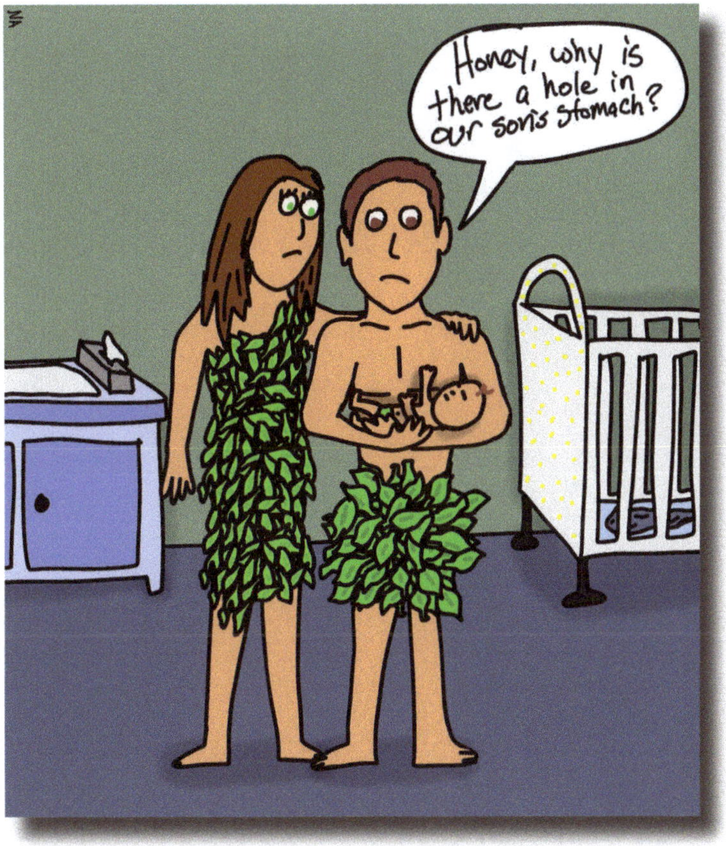
Honey, why is there a hole in our son's stomach?

Adam and Eve discover belly buttons.

It had been 45 minutes since service ended and Billy's parents were still talking; he wasn't sure if he'd ever see home again.

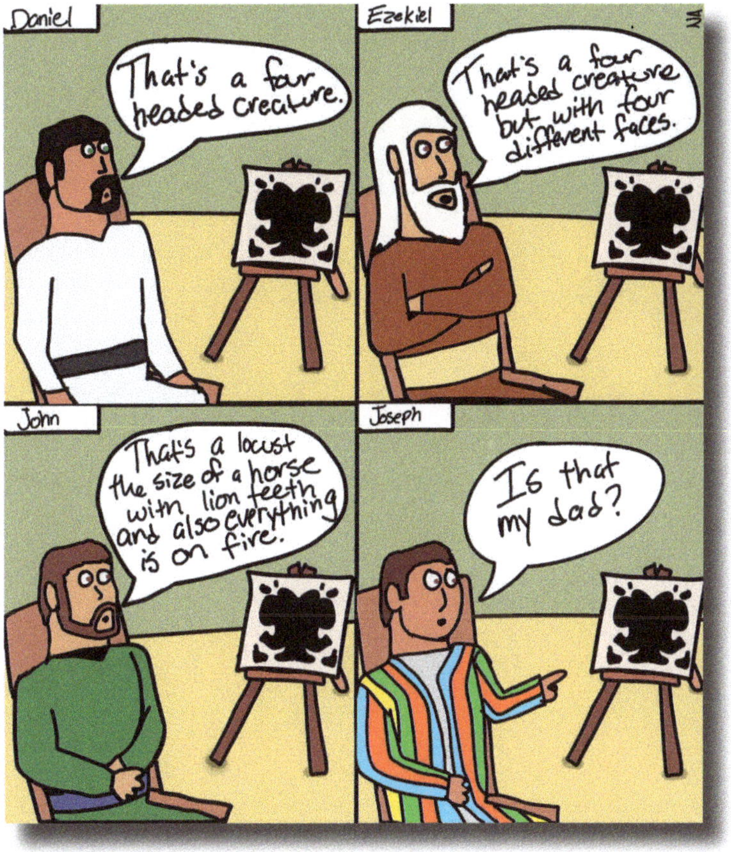
Daniel
That's a four headed creature.
Ezekiel
That's a four headed creature but with four different faces.
John
That's a locust the size of a horse with lion teeth and also everything is on fire.
Joseph
Is that my dad?

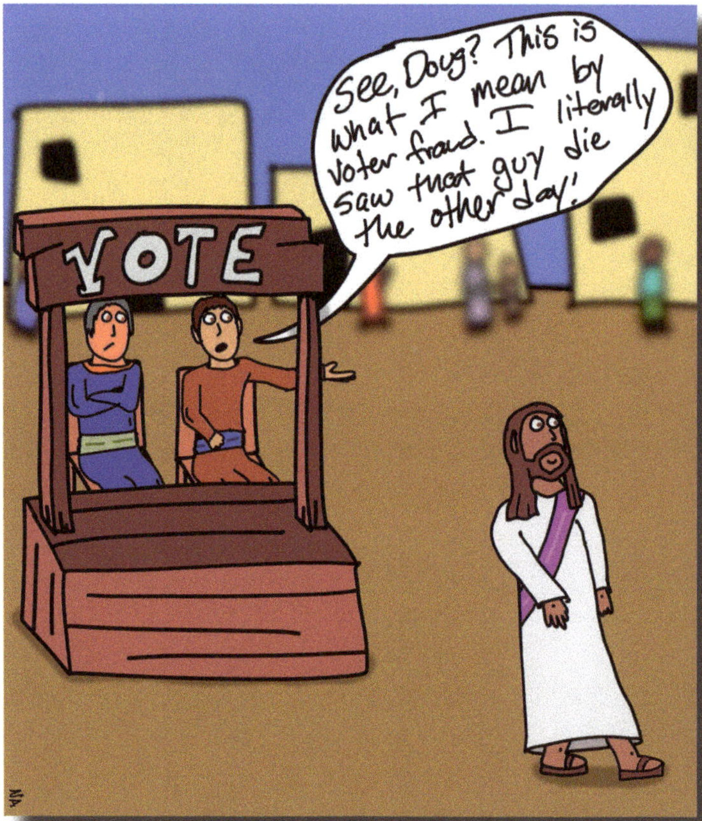
See, Doug? This is what I mean by voter fraud. I literally saw that guy die the other day!
VOTE

Confusingly enough for Jerusalem's poll workers, Super Tuesday immediately followed Easter Monday.

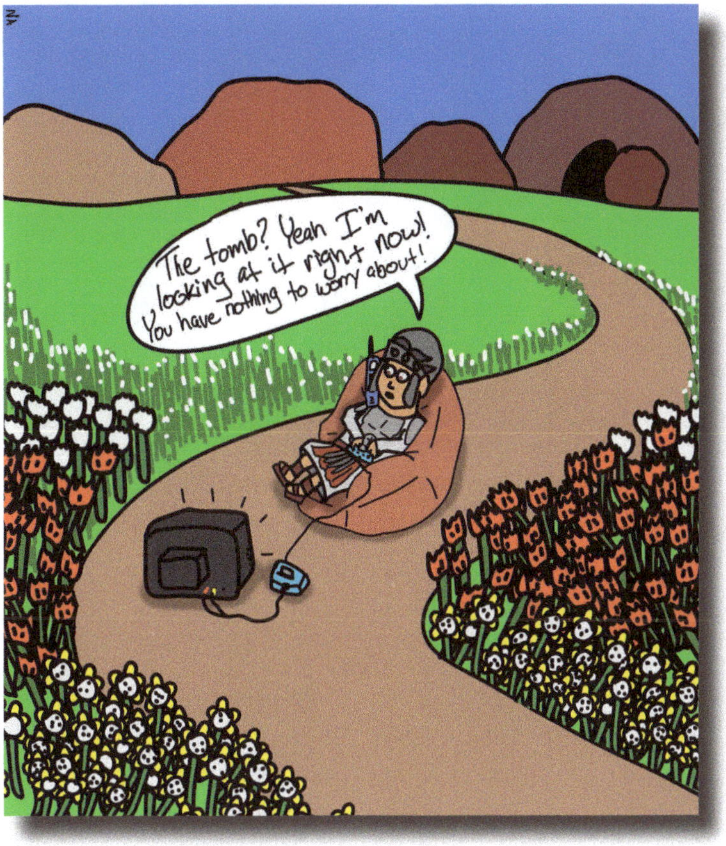
The tomb? Yeah I'm looking at it right now! You have nothing to worry about!

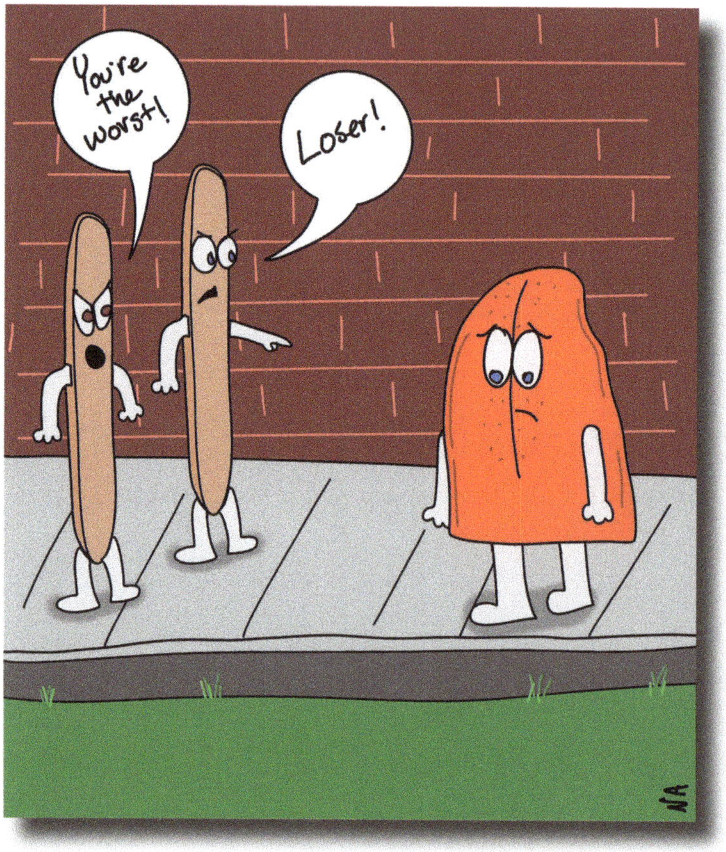
You're the worst!
Loser!
NA

Tongue depressors.

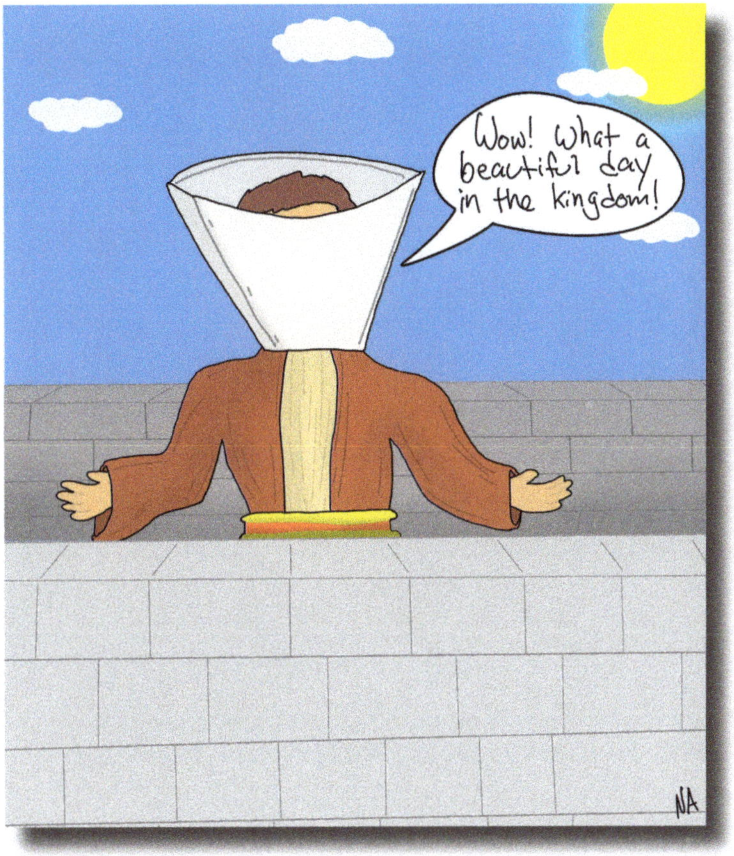
Wow! What a beautiful day in the kingdom!

King David wasn't taking any more chances.

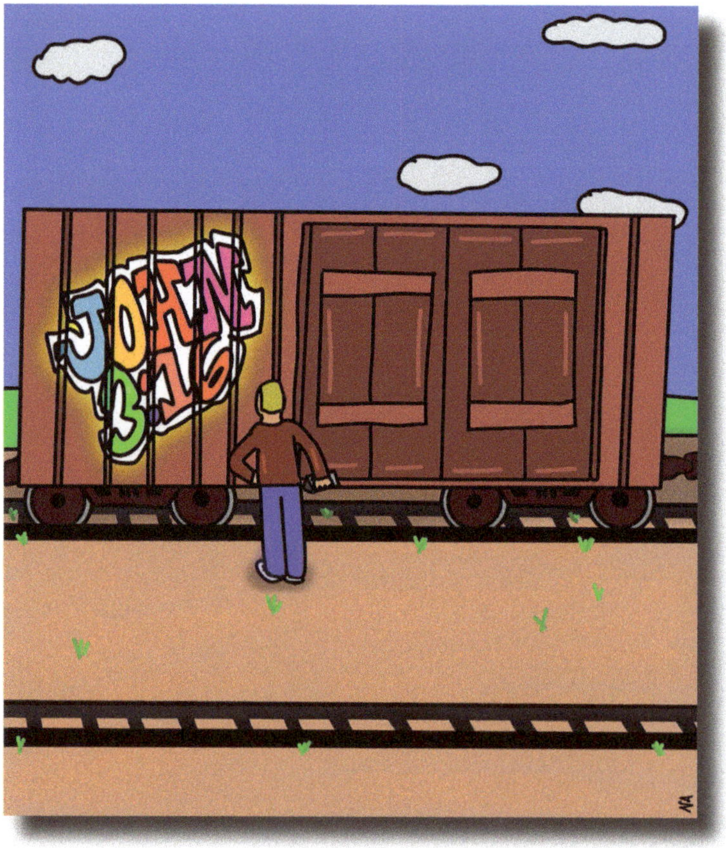
JOHN 3:16

Evandalism.

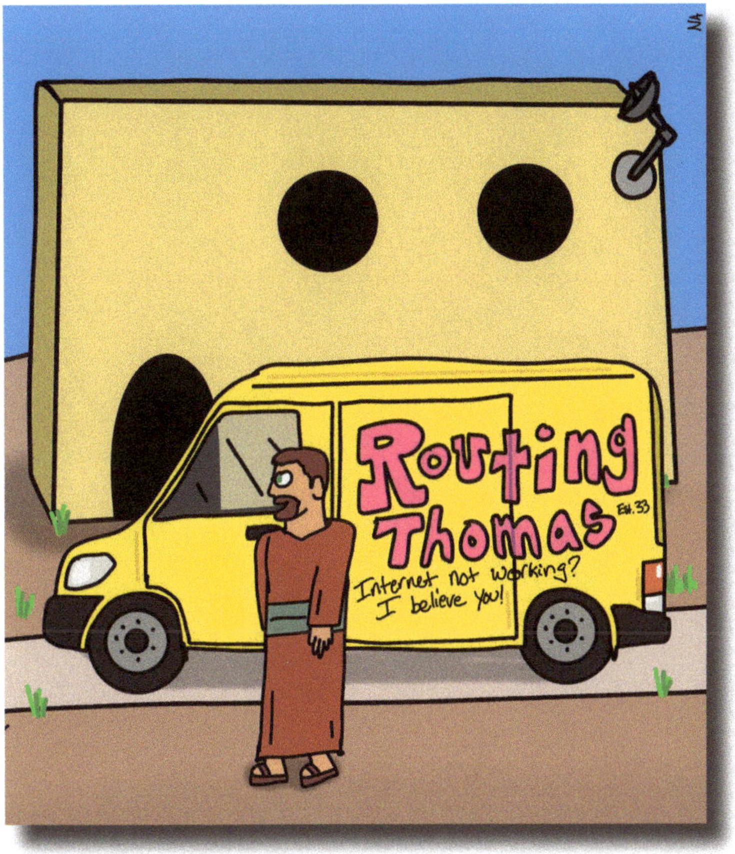
Routing Thomas
Est. 33
Internet not working?
I believe you!

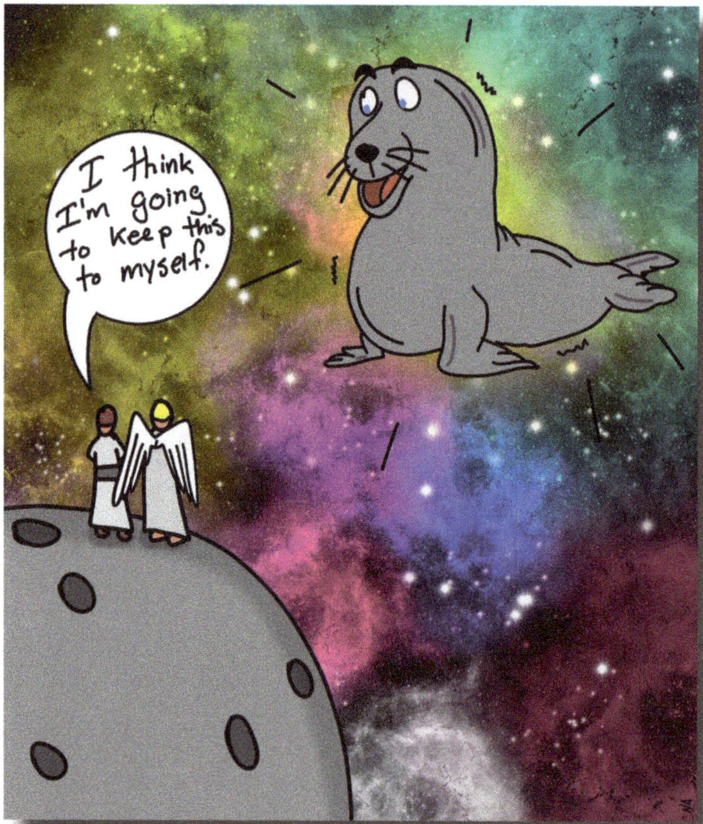
I think I'm going to keep this to myself.

John the Revelator decides not to include the eighth seal.

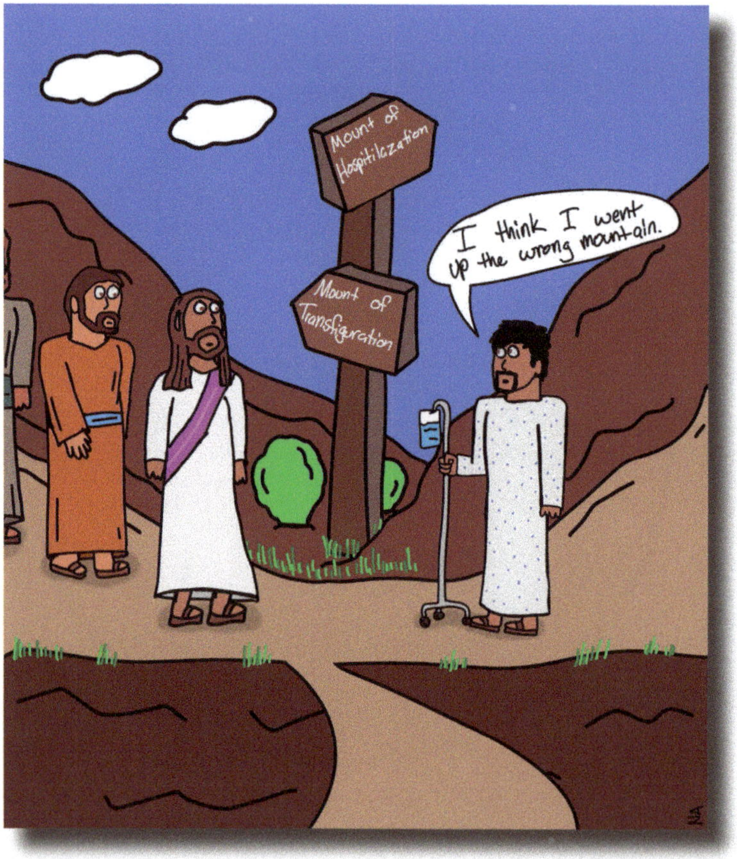
Mount of Hospitilazation
Mount of Transfiguration
I think I went up the wrong mountain.

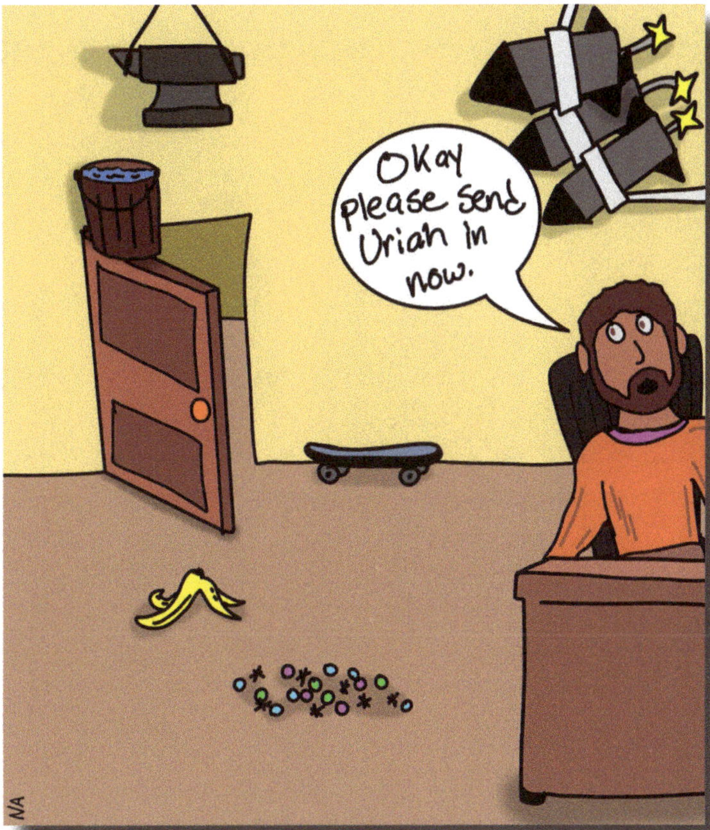
Okay please send Uriah in now.
NA

Initially, King David could not figure out what to do with Uriah.

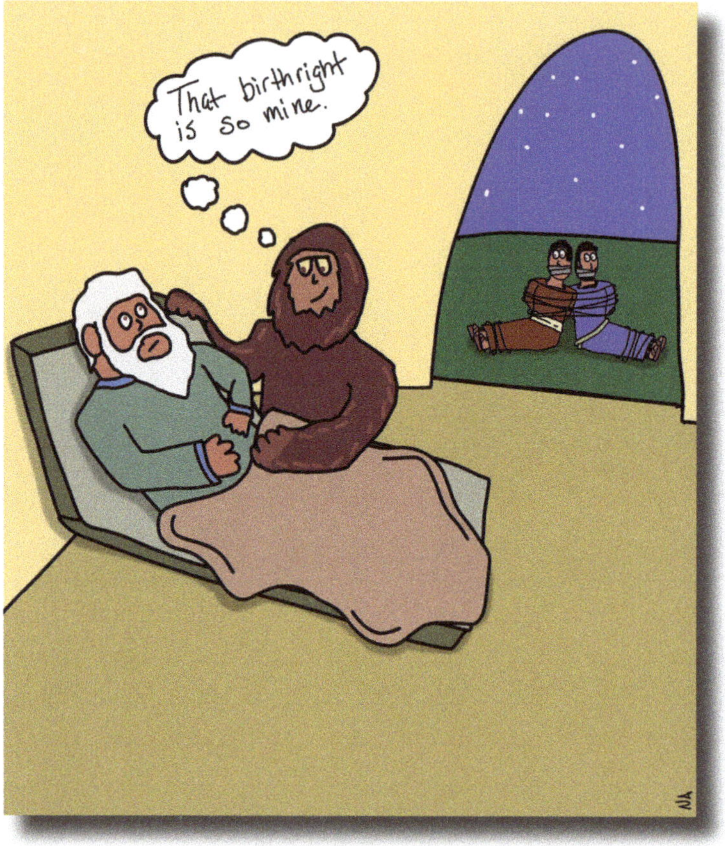
That birthright is so mine.

At the last moment, Big Foot stepped in, stole Jacob's idea, and walked off with the birthright.

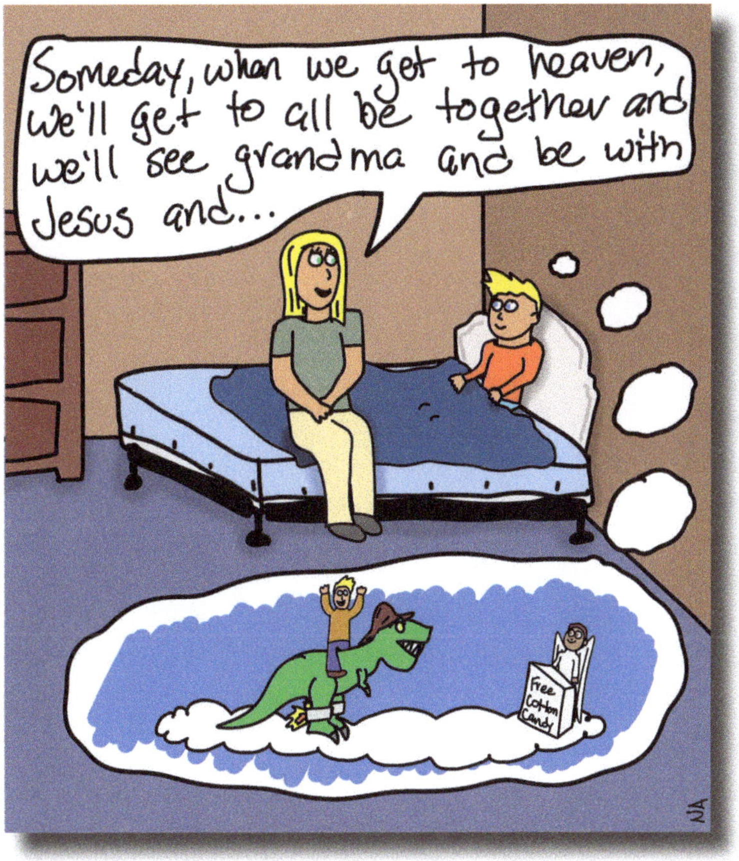
Someday, when we get to heaven, we'll get to all be together and we'll see grandma and be with Jesus and...
Free Cotton Candy
NA

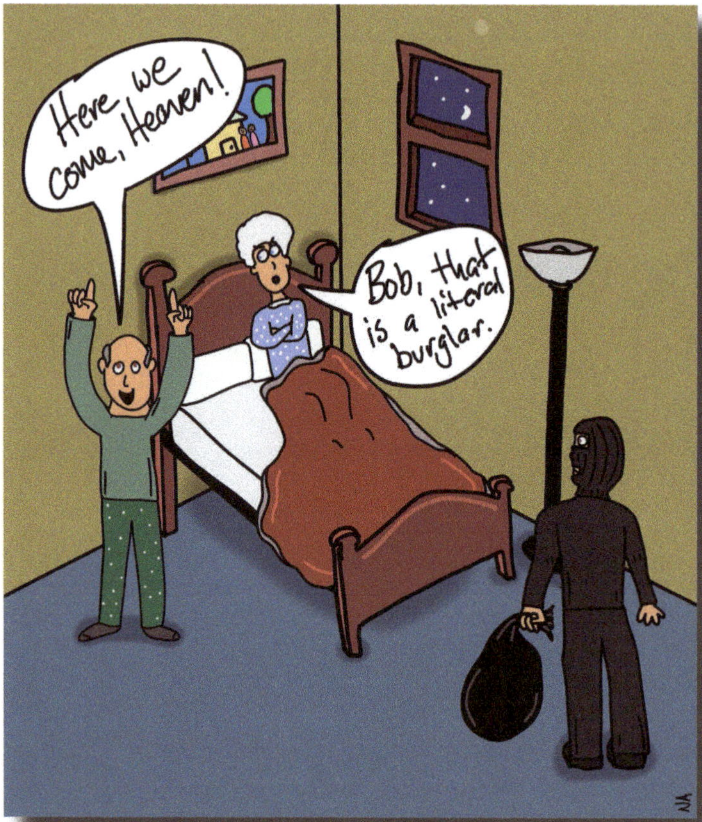
Here we come, Heaven!
Bob, that is a literal burglar.

Bob completely misunderstands
1 Thessalonians 5:2.

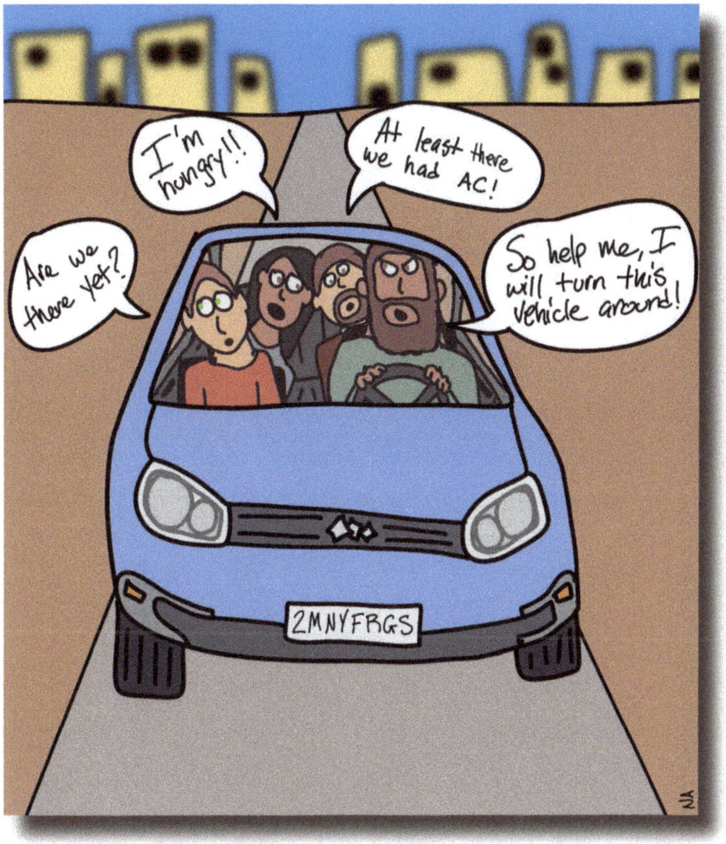
I'm hungry!!
At least there we had AC!
Are we there yet?
So help me, I will turn this vehicle around!
2MNYFRGS

Moses had barely left Egypt with the Israelites when they started complaining.

"Joshua, get up onto this couch, for the floor you're standing on is lava."

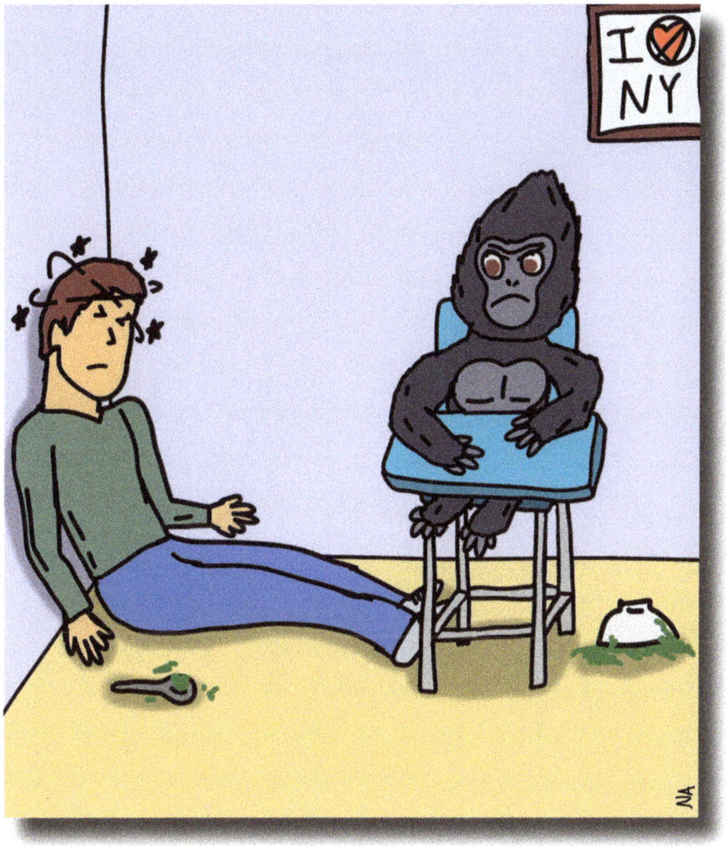
I ♥ NY

Babysitting was going great until Jeremy tried
"Here comes the plane" with Baby Kong.

Tommy's parents thought the fully illustrated Bible was a great gift until they realized that it included Song of Solomon.

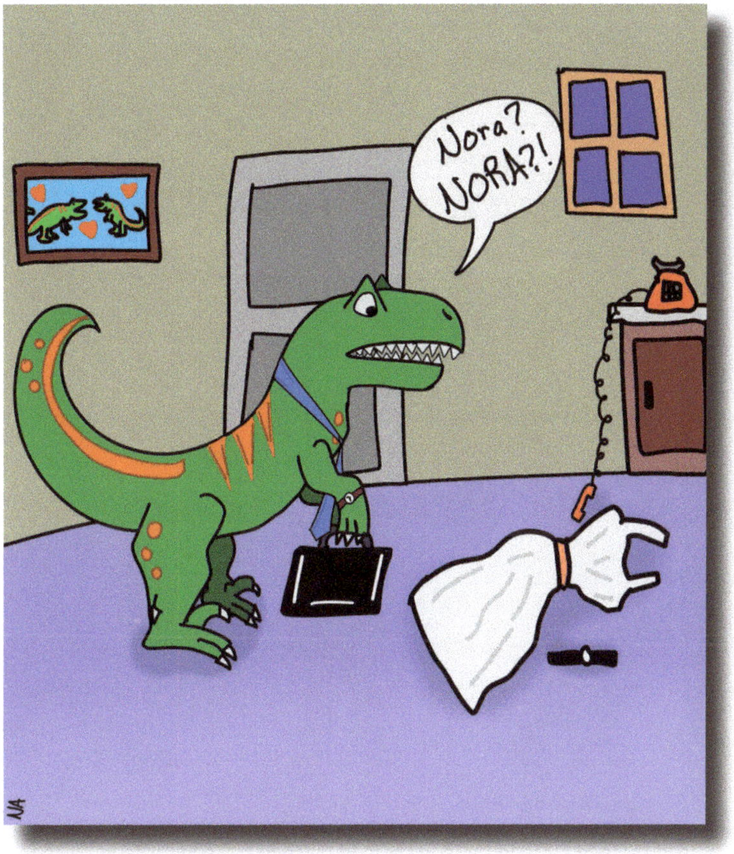
Nora?
NORA?!

Velocirapture.

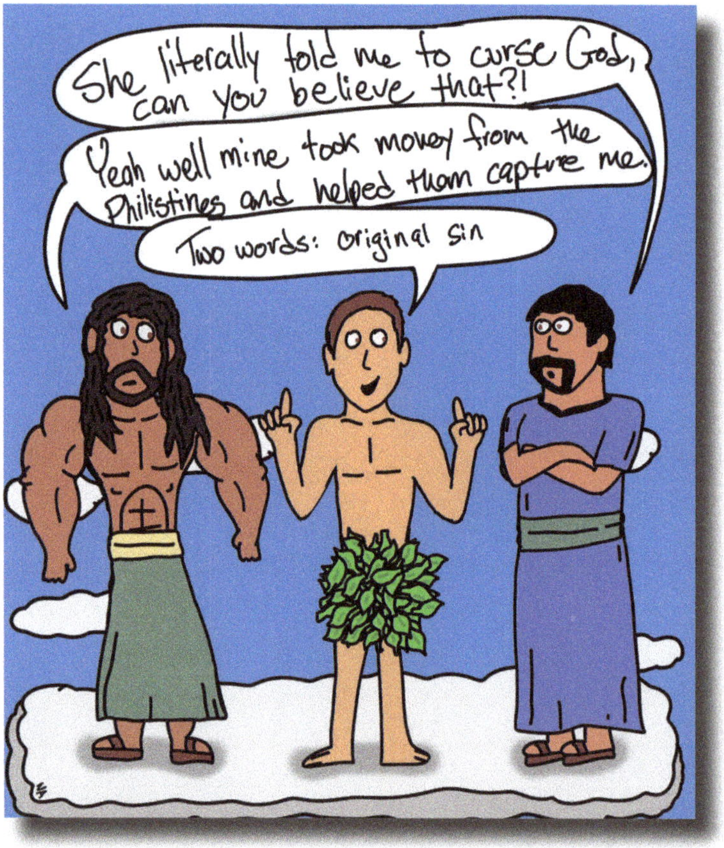
She literally told me to curse God, can you believe that?!
Yeah well mine took money from the Philistines and helped them capture me.
Two words: original sin

Woman troubles.

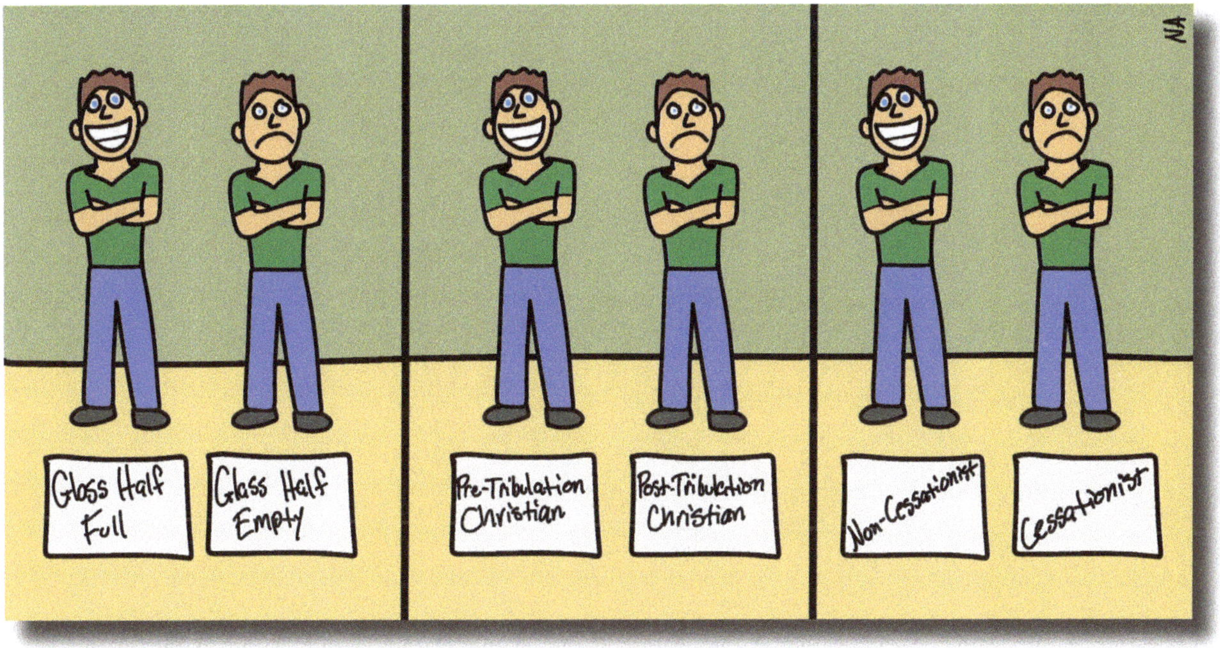
Glass Half Full
Glass Half Empty
Pre-Tribulation Christian
Post-Tribulation Christian
Non-Cessationist
Cessationist
NJA

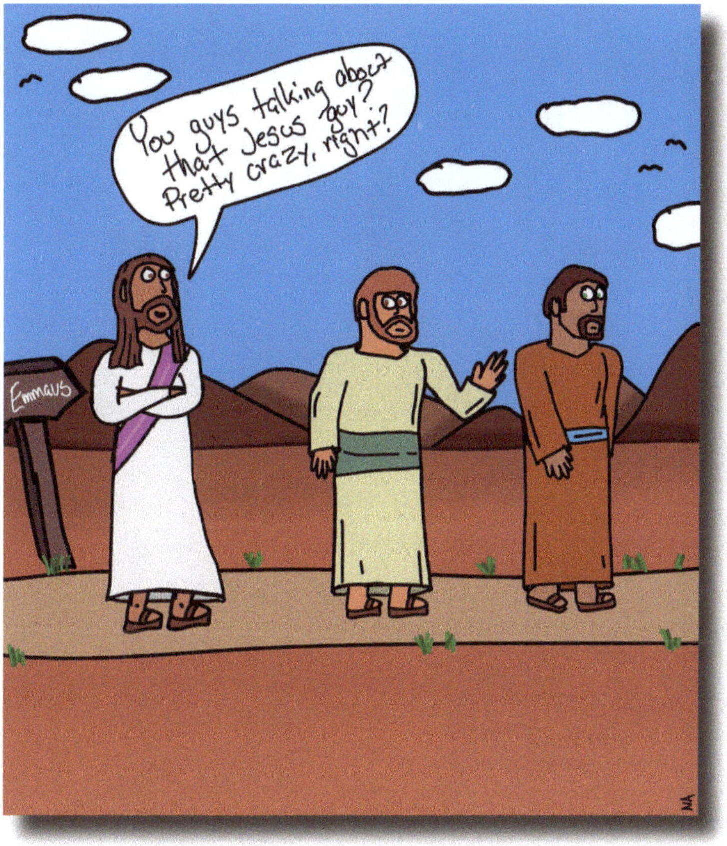
You guys talking about that Jesus guy? Pretty crazy, right?
Emmaus

On this week's episode of Undercover Boss.

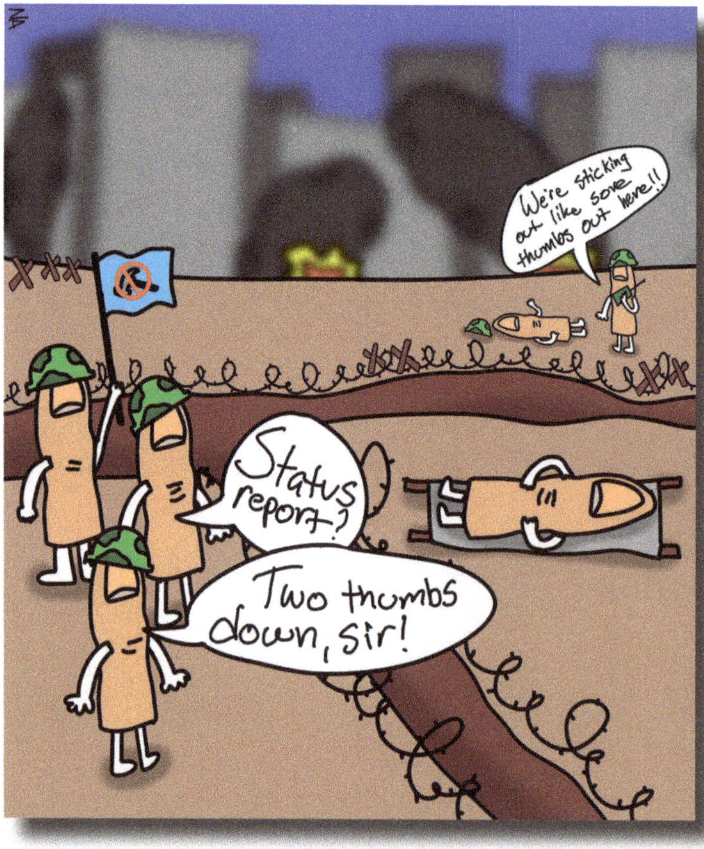
We're sticking out like sore thumbs out here!!
Status report?
Two thumbs down, sir!

Thumb war.

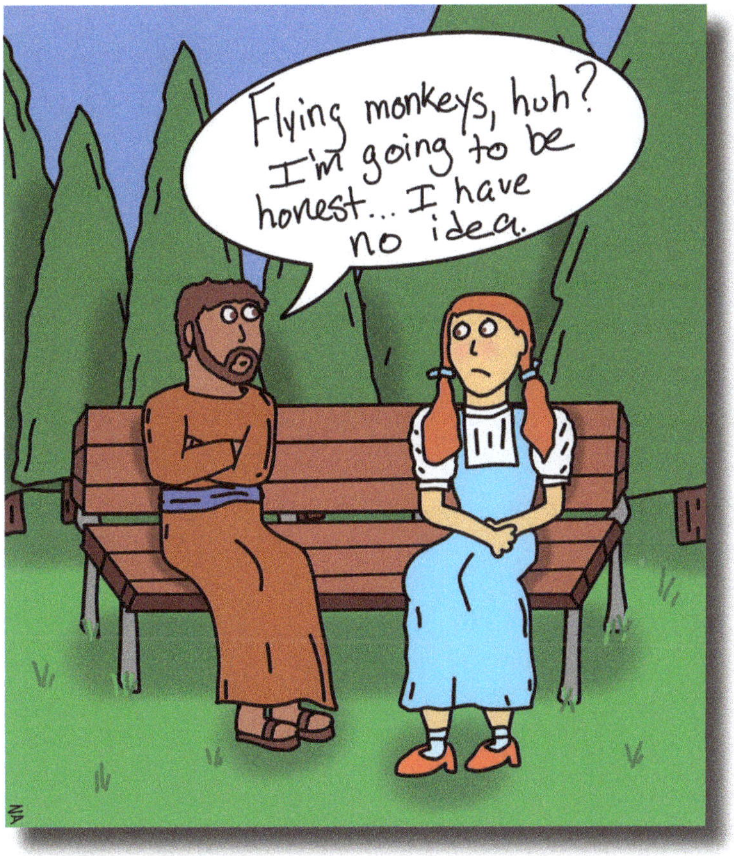
Flying monkeys, huh? I'm going to be honest... I have no idea.

Joseph takes a crack at Dorothy's dream.

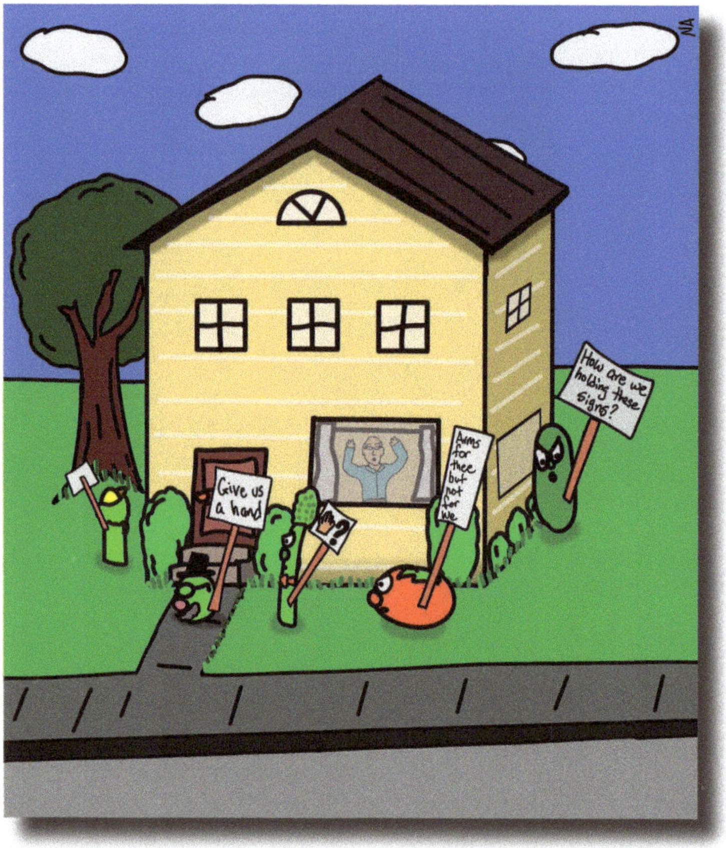
NA
Give us a hand
?
Arms for thee but not for we
How are we holding these signs?

Unable to wear watches or participate in high fives, the famed sentient vegetation decide to protest outside the house of the show's creator for their right to bear arms.

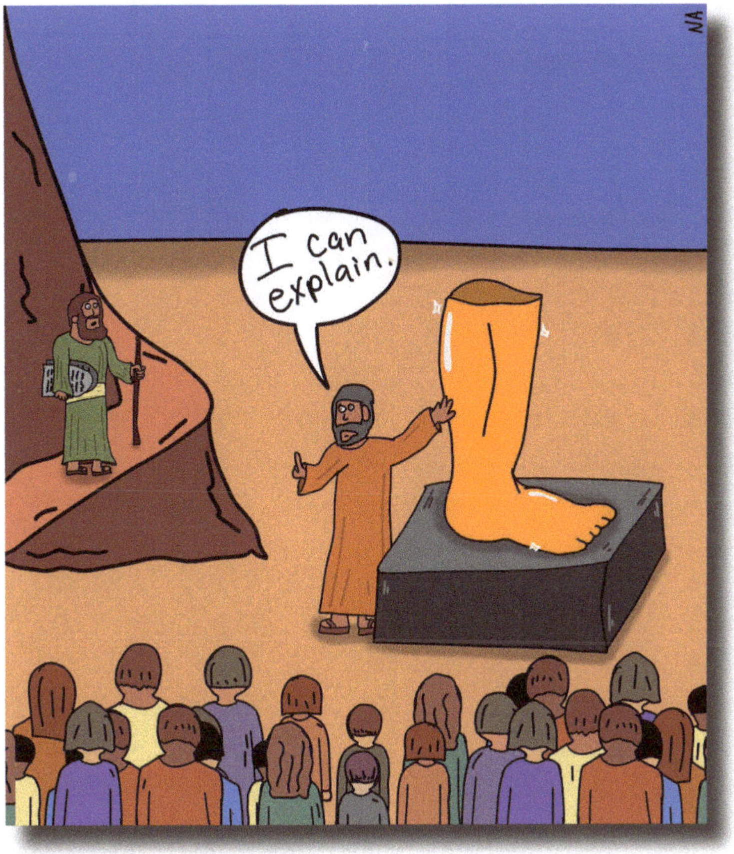
I can explain.

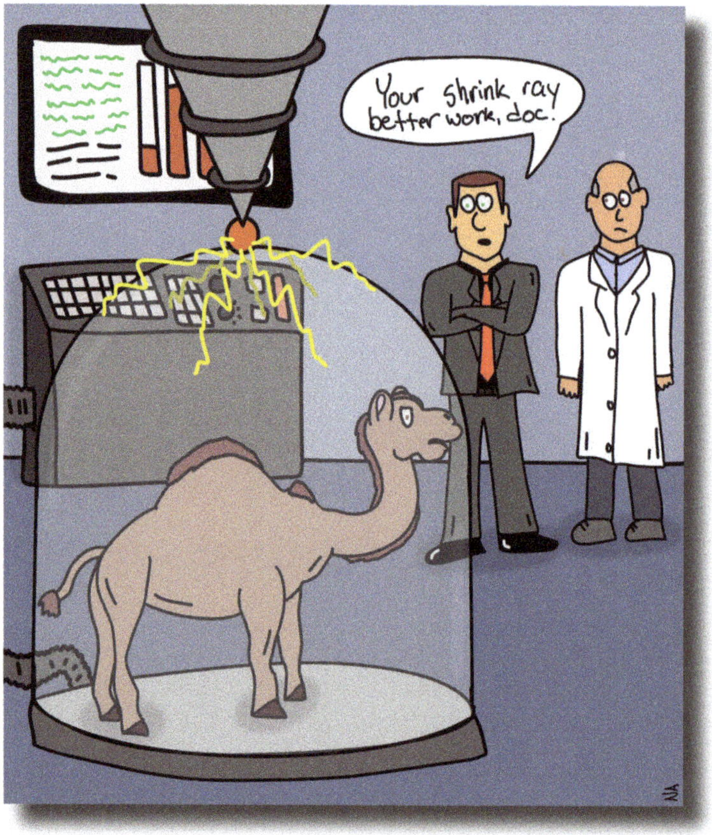
Your shrink ray better work, doc!

Televangelist hires team of scientists to do the impossible.

The Marriage Supper of the Lamb was a dream come true for Sister Doris, whose Meat Stroganoff was a potluck legend back on earth.

Scotcharoos Recipe

Ingredients:

1 cup corn syrup
1 cup sugar
5 cups crisp rice cereal
1.5 cups peanut butter
1 cup chocolate chips
1 cup butterscotch chips

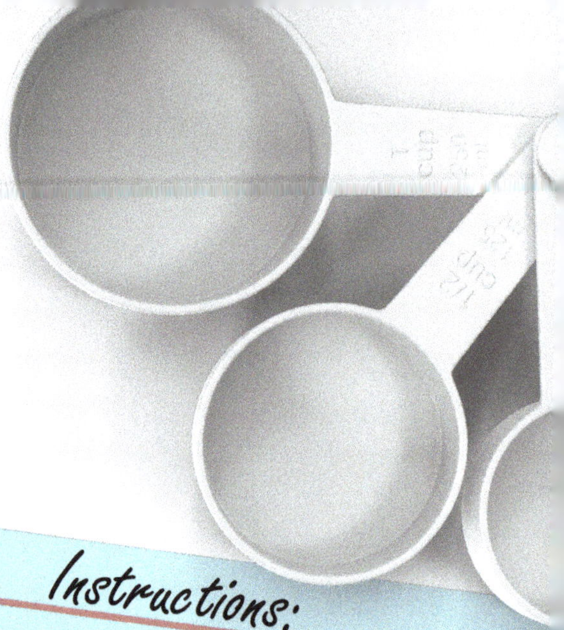

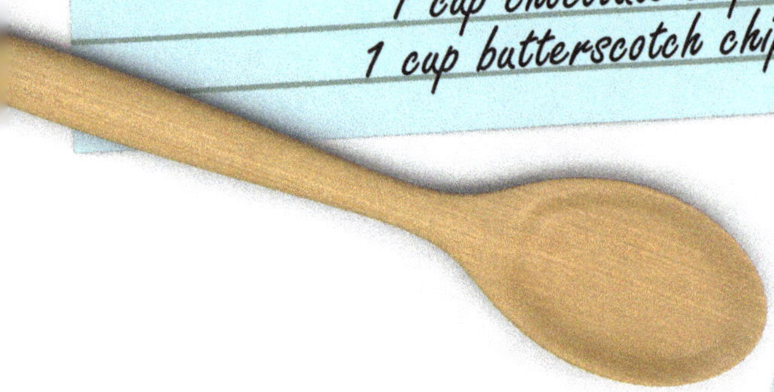

Instructions:

1. Combine the corn syrup and sugar in a saucepan on medium-low heat and bring to light boil for about a minute.
2. Add the peanut butter to it and begin stirring the ingredients together until smooth.
3. Pour mixture over crisp rice in bowl and mix until evenly coated.
4. Pour mixture into parchment lined dish and lightly pack it down using spatula.
5. Melt the chocolate and butterscotch chips in the microwave for thirty seconds at a time.
6. Once completely melted, pour over top and spread evenly across bars.

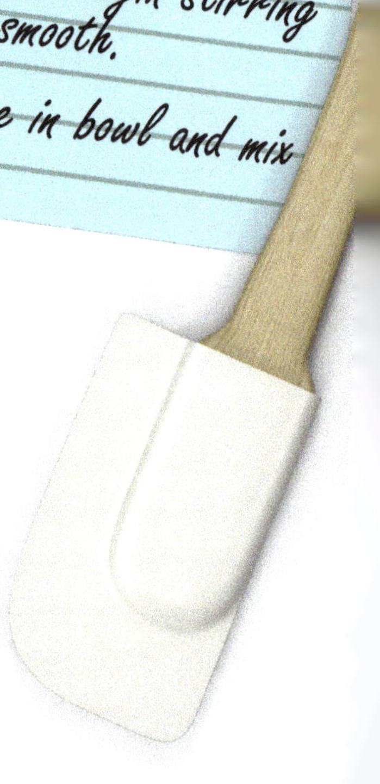

www.ingramcontent.com/pod-product-compliance
Lightning Source LLC
LaVergne TN
LVHW070533070526
838199LV00075B/6774